RADICAL
DISCIPLESHIP

RADICAL DISCIPLESHIP

by

STEPHEN A. BLY

MOODY PRESS

CHICAGO

to jan . . . thanks

Contents

1

But, Lord, I Just Want to Be Great

I am a frustrated Christian. Are you?

Here is what I mean. I have been told by thoughtful, mature, and very spiritual friends that I should dedicate myself to serving the Lord with all my gifts, talents, and abilities.

"God deserves your very best effort," I am told. I believe them. So off I charge on my valiant white horse to do battle with the enemies of His Kingdom. So far, so good.

The problem comes when I begin to consider what will happen after the battle. If I fail miserably I will be branded as a spiritual weakling—too tangled in sin and rebellion to be of much benefit to God's work in the world. If I barely fail, I will be considered merely a lazy servant, not willing to give all it takes to succeed. If I barely push past the halfway mark in the winner's column, I will be reminded of how close the victory was and how coincidental the circumstances proved to be.

On the other hand, if I reach my goal—if I score a smashing success—some thoughtful, mature, and very spiritual friends will remind me that the glory of victory belongs to God alone. They will insinuate that my victory came only by some self-seeking, self-glorifying promotion—something that no conscientious Christian would ever give in to. My smashing victory becomes a spiritual blunder. I am a frustrated Christian.

Sally Stewart, a young housewife and mother, is a frustrated Christian too. She quit teaching school last year when Brian was born. Sally's husband, Bill, is a fireman whose work schedule leaves Sally alone with some extra time several days a week. She wanted very much to get together with other young mothers

9

to share problems and needs and ideas. Because Sally is a very committed Christian, she felt compelled to communicate the good news of Jesus Christ to others. She decided to start a weekly young mothers' group, where friendship and faith could be mutually exchanged. Sally's neighbor, Debbie, was interested also, even though she was not a Christian. Debbie had been a prayer concern of Sally's for two years. Debbie was interested in crafts—a real strawflower, découpage, and macramé nut. So the two concocted a plan whereby they would invite others over for crafts and goodies and an occasional devotional by Sally.

They began to spread word around the neighborhood about this new Happy Homemakers group. They put a notice in the church page of the weekly shopper, and they even contacted the neighborhood preschool for possible interest.

On Wednesday morning at nine o'clock there were six other girls besides Sally and Debbie. They were thrilled, but the day turned out to be a disaster. Eight little squirming, playful, fighting cherubs ruled and reigned.

"Next week," announced Sally, "we'll get a babysitter for the children."

Sally secured the junior high room at the church and someone to watch the kids. It was just the right combination. The next week there were ten ladies, and in two more weeks there were eighteen. Most were non-Christians, yet they never seemed to mind Sally's devotional time.

However, eighteen women meant twenty-six children, and soon complaints about what was happening to the junior high room were heard at church meetings.

"It would be all right if there weren't so many," said one person.

"Well, it would be all right if it were a regular church program, but sitting around pasting Christmas card holders is not my idea of the type of spiritual program we should support," another chimed in.

The board decided that the junior high room, otherwise used only on Sunday mornings, would no longer be available to the

Happy Homemakers. Sally was just too successful. Too bad. Sally is a frustrated Christian.

So is Don. Last night was Don's first attempt at public speaking at the Christian Men's Club where he related his story of how Christ had saved him and changed his whole philosophy of the hardware business. He had planned on the talk for weeks. Each story, illustration, and joke was carefully chosen. He knew just when to be serious and when to relax. His words and thoughts were memorized. He even practiced in front of a mirror. It was a lot of preparation, but he was determined to do the very best job he knew how.

That preparation paid off. The audience seemed to thoroughly enjoy Don's talk. They cried when he wanted them to cry, and they grinned when he wanted them to grin. They seemed to follow every thought and to understand every story. When he concluded his remarks, there were cheers and applause and a good number of "amens." Don at once felt satisfied. He had wanted a sense of satisfaction in doing something for the Lord, and now he had it.

He was inwardly pleased and praising the Lord as he and Peggy stepped out of the Memorial Building on their way to the car. The clouds covered the stars and made the parking lot even darker than normal. As they reached their car, he overheard a couple walking behind them.

The husband said to his wife, "Well, I still say it was too flamboyant and slick. Why, you'd think he was trying to sell us all a new lawn mower. Just another glory-seeking salesman jumping onto the gospel bandwagon, I suppose."

Don was crushed, frustrated. His speaking ministry was shelved for quite a long time. He had oversucceeded.

Success is one frustration many Christians face, not because they cannot achieve it but rather because too many secular and "sacred" friends believe that success is somehow un-Christian. If you do not think this is true, just listen to the local ministerial group talk about the "super" churches in your area. You will hear comments about shallow theology, gimmick promotions, and the like, but little is said about their phenomenal success at converting people.

There is a second and equally strong drive that tends to frustrate many an industrious servant of the Lord. Success in itself is a shallow and temporary achievement, but *success with a purpose*—that is where meaning and satisfaction come in.

Several years ago I found I possessed all of the elements of the "Great American Dream" (loving wife, happy kids, challenging job, comfortable home, etc.). Yet I had a gnawing feeling that something was missing. I felt a sense of apathy as if I had entered into a magic cycle that would repeat itself week after week after week until my life ended. This is when I discovered God (or should I say, He manifested Himself to me). He was the element missing in my cycle of life, and through my faith in Christ He is missing no more.

In all truthfulness it was only a matter of a few years (or was it a few months?) until I settled into a sacred, rather than a secular, rut. The cycle of meetings, services, and volunteer projects added many hours of activity to my life but not necessarily the knowledge that my life was worthwhile, making a lasting impact on my community and world.

I believe mine is a common frustration. All at once it dawns on us: Are we doing anything of lasting value? Sure, we are busy, but is what we are doing really worthwhile? I mean, ten years from now will it matter that I spent two hours debating the trustees over whether to put camelhide tan or avocado green carpeting in the youth chapel? Will we even have any youth in ten years? Will my "Jesus Saves" Christmas lights have any eternal value on my neighbor who is struggling through a sticky divorce? Will my screaming every Wednesday afternoon for fifteen fifth graders to settle down and memorize their Bible verses really have a dramatic, lasting, positive effect on their young lives?

Perhaps. But I want to know! I want to succeed. I want to succeed at something meaningful. I do not want to abandon any responsibilities. I want to know first that it is OK, acceptable, approved Christian behavior to succeed, and, second, that what is accomplished will be of lasting effect and importance.

Am I chasing an ever-fading mirage? a bubble that can only explode in my face? I do not think so.

If we note the example of Jesus, and I know all Christians have some desire to do this, we will find that He had no fear of excellence. One of the most powerful and dramatic verses in the New Testament is Mark 7:37, where the utterly astonished crowd exclaims: "He has done all things well!" Success and excellence are His common standards of performance, and He never lowers those standards for a moment.

The wedding at Cana was a joyous occasion. Jesus and His disciples—and a mixture of curiosity seekers, undoubtedly—found their way to the celebration. Naturally, with such large numbers of guests, some of whom were perhaps unexpected, the host soon ran out of wine. At that point, Jesus turned the entire water reservoir (six twenty-five-gallon jugs) into fine wine. That was at least 150 gallons of wine—enough to satisfy the thirst of the entire village, let alone the wedding guests! Jesus oversucceeded. He does all things well.

Later in His ministry He faced the dilemma of feeding five thousand hungry men and their families. In the miracle of the loaves He not only insured that all would have plenty, but also provided for twelve big basketfuls to be left over. He overprovided. Jesus does all things well.

Once when He was busy teaching the followers, He was abruptly interrupted by the purposeful destruction of the ceiling above Him. Through the haze of a roomful of dust he saw a paralyzed man being let down to Him. The crowd immediately sensed the need of the moment and awaited Jesus' words of healing. Certainly a quick healing would be all that was needed, to please both the paralytic and the crowd, but merely stopping with the healing would have been doing only half the job. So the first words from Jesus were startling: "My son, your sins are forgiven." Then and only then was the man healed. Jesus knew the man's needs. He not only succeeded, but He succeeded with a lasting purpose. Jesus does all things well.

An equally important teaching from Jesus deals directly with the area of greatness. (I like to define greatness as success with a purpose.) Jesus' followers, most of whom would be canonized as saints, spent a lot of time arguing about which one of them was the greatest. They mentally divided up the spoils of the Kingdom and argued over imaginary places of honor. When Jesus got wind of their ambition, He did not squelch it with blistering tirades about the evils of greatness, nor did He force them to submit to a stringent discipline of forced humility. Instead, in Mark 10:43 we hear Him say,"Whoever wishes to become great among you shall be your servant."

Jesus gave a basic blueprint for greatness. To find success with a purpose (that is, greatness) is a basic drive in most people. Rather than trying to suppress that drive, Jesus channeled it in the right direction.

That leads me to the purpose of this book. I want you to discover spiritual principles for experiencing greatness and how they apply to our lives. Greatness in its highest and noblest form will have a lasting impact on our world. In short, I want you to know how to make your mark in life.

2

Join the Way-Paver Society

John the Baptist was Jesus' idea of a great man. He said of him: ". . . Among those born of women, there is no one greater than John . . ." (Luke 7:28). John rates as high as Moses, Elijah, Daniel, and the like. Yet we know John's ministry was short (three years at the most) and ended with his imprisonment and beheading. We do not even have record that he ever performed a miracle! How did John find greatness? What was his secret?

First, John the Baptist knew his mission in life. He knew specifically what he had to do and how to do it. John was a preacher with a message to proclaim. His message was simple and direct. "Repent, for the kingdom of heaven is at hand." It is a clear, positive message, couched in terms all could understand. He offered no apology for his blunt pronouncements. Why? Because his message was helpful and encouraging.

If you were pleasantly sailing down a river, having a picnic with good friends and enjoying the beauty of a clear, fresh spring day, the anxious shouts of a bystander on the riverbank might be very annoying. If he were shouting, "Stop! Stop! Turn around! I don't want you to go that way!" we would shake our heads in disgust thinking, *There's someone who really wants to spoil our day. What a negative person.* Yet if he were warning of a treacherous 100-foot waterfall just around the next bend, and someone had sense enough to listen and paddle to shore, then we would consider that a very positive, encouraging warning. The serious disciple need never think he is being negative by giving the message, "Repent and turn."

15

John's message to the religious leaders was even more pointed. With fearless, even reckless abandon, he pronounced God's judgment against the Sadducees and Pharisees. He had a great desire for them to understand clearly what God was saying. They had been trusting in their physical descendency from Abraham to keep them in good standing with God. They considered themselves special, chosen ones. John told them plainly that they were no more chosen than the rocks beneath their feet, and that they too must humble themselves as the others had.

John's message to Herod, king of Galilee, was equally clear and to the point. He called him to account for his immoral claims on his brother's wife. That was bound to cause repercussions. John was arrested and finally beheaded. Some might say his message was too clear, but none can doubt that John knew his mission.

The second factor in the greatness of John the Baptist was his constant awareness of his position in relationship to Jesus. He said of Him, "After me comes One who is mightier than I, and I am not even fit to stoop down and untie the thong of His sandals." When they tried to confer upon him higher honor than was due him, he stated clearly, "I am not the Christ. . . . I am a voice of one crying in the wilderness, 'MAKE STRAIGHT THE WAY OF THE LORD,' as Isaiah the prophet said."

Even when it meant losing some of his closest followers, John did not hesitate to point them to Christ. John was always aware of his subordination to the Lord.

The third factor in John's greatness was his refusal to let personal motives and successes divert him from either his position or his mission. In John 3:22-30 there is an overlapping of the ministries of John and Jesus. Both were preaching and baptizing in the upper Jordan River valley. When it was pointed out by some of John's disciples that Jesus was drawing bigger crowds, John reminded them that his job was to carry out his mission regardless of the numbers of people involved. "A man can receive nothing, unless it has been given him from heaven." He also made clear that he would always be subordinate in position, for Jesus was the bridegroom and John merely the best man.

John's humility in greatness can best be seen in the powerful statement: "He must increase, but I must decrease."

John's role, then, was to be a way-paver. He paved the way for others to reach Christ. He also preceded Jesus, preparing the way for His ministry to follow. If we are determined to follow John's pathway to success with a purpose, we must learn to be way-pavers.

The first lesson is basic. If we want to be in the business of pointing others to Jesus, obviously we must know the way ourselves. Every time I drive through San Francisco I get lost. My otherwise keen sense of direction gets left on the Oakland Bay Bridge, or on the Peninsula, or somewhere else. I once asked a pedestrian how to get back on the freeway that goes across the Golden Gate Bridge. He began with a complicated "up two signals, turn left (or is it right?), then down three blocks, hang a right past the tower, and then two blocks, or maybe six blocks north. You can't miss it."

"Are you sure?" I asked.

"Well, I think so," replied the man. "Of course, I'm only a tourist here myself."

"Have you ever been there?" I asked.

"Oh, not yet," he replied, "but I overheard the bellhop tell the man next to me in the elevator."

I didn't want hearsay; I wanted concrete advice from one who had been there.

The first, fundamental, indispensable step toward success with a purpose is knowing Jesus Christ as your personal Lord and Savior. A great number of Christians who know Him still have trouble explaining how they "got there" and therefore are unable to be of much help pointing others down the trail. A successful way-paver must not only know the way himself, but he must also be familiar enough with the route that he can direct another.

Every denomination and Christian organization I know of has material designed to help you tell others how to find a meaningful relationship with the Lord. Secure and use this material. You should memorize the basic elements of the gospel so that you can be fully prepared to give accurate information when needed. First Corinthians 15:3-8 might be a place to begin. Also, have in mind the process of simply telling in your own language how you personally came to know Him as Lord and Savior.

How about beginning to taste what it is like to be a way-paver? Make a list of five people you desire most to come to the Lord. Be specific with names. Do not put down "my friends" or "my family"; rather, use their names.

1. _____

2. _____

3. _____

4. _____

5. _____

The second step in paving the way for others to reach Jesus is to remove the obstacles that hinder their progress. Raesh Makil was a young Hindu student studying in our country. I wanted very much to have him find a relationship with the Lord. He had heard the gospel message many times before. I gave it to him again. I told him my personal testimony. Yet he was in no way ready to become a Christian. He had a long list of personal hurts and hassles from the past that he wanted desperately to talk about with someone who cared.

I listened, and I listened, and I listened. For one whole weekend and through several letters and phone calls I listened. Then one night I received a call from Raesh. He had unintentionally found himself in a church meeting and while there had accepted Jesus as his Savior. The big obstacles and heartaches of the past had finally been removed from his pathway to the Lord. My role had been merely helping to remove those obstacles.

What are some of the more common obstacles preventing people from coming to Christ?

"I'm just too busy." Many think about becoming a Christian in the way they think of writing a will. "Oh, I really need to do it. I will do it someday, honest. But I'm so tied up with other things now. It will just have to wait."

"I tried it once, but . . ." Or, "If you only knew how rotten my past is." As if the matter were settled and hopeless.

"I'm afraid of what I might have to give up, or what I might have to do." These people wrongly think that they would be surrendering to a life of misery.

"I'm too ill to think about it right now." Some wrongly suppose that wholeness is the only state acceptable for approaching God.

"I really don't know enough about it." Others imply that salvation is only for the educated.

"I know better than to believe all that mystical stuff about religion." These vainly trust their extremely fallible logic to lead them.

"What difference will it make, anyway?" Many incorrectly suppose that we will all end up in the same condition anyway.

A way-paver is constantly in the process of removing obstacles such as these:

- time   Encourage them to set priorities, to do the truly important things.

- past   Listen to their heartaches, failures, and worries.

- fear   Love them and show them your complete trust in God.

- health   Help them back to health and encourage them to come to God just as they are.

- ignorance   Inform them; tell them all they need to know in order to find Jesus as Savior.

- pseudo-   Reason with them. Christianity does make
  intelligence   sense; it is rational. Challenge them to a
                   faith commitment.

- lethargy   Push them off dead center. Do not let them
                   sit there and rot.

The following planner might help you get started as a way-paver.

Those who need obstacles removed on their way to Jesus	What are the obstacles? (Find out!)	What can I personally do to help remove obstacles?	By what date will I have it done?
1. _____	_____	_____	_____
2. _____	_____	_____	_____
3. _____	_____	_____	_____
4. _____	_____	_____	_____
5. _____	_____	_____	_____
6. _____	_____	_____	_____

The third mark of a truly great way-paver is the ability and desire to get everything ready for someone else's ministry. John the Baptist gathered and prepared the crowds, then he turned them over to Jesus. John was the advance man.

In the days when the circus coming to town was the year's most exciting event, the most important person was the advance man. He would arrive in town a week or two early. It was his job to see that the posters got put up, the proper permits were secured, and the newspaper received the right publicity. In short, he built up the anticipation of the town so that when the great and glorious day arrived, the streets were lined with cheering people. Just about everyone in town was there, everyone except the advance man, of course. He was busy in the next town, arranging for the following week's performance.

Paul certainly knew the advantages of having an advance man in the ministry. In 2 Corinthians 9 he writes of a case in which he ensures that a proper offering is collected before he arrives to send to the poor saints in Jerusalem.

Are you paving the way for another's ministry?

Is your car crammed full of neighbors each Sunday as you go to church?

Are you volunteering your time to babysit so that others might be out visiting the sick and needy or enjoying a deserved break?

Are you donating time to your church office so your church leaders have more time for "prayer and the ministry of the Word"?

Are you inviting all the children on your block over to your house so that someone can come in and teach a Bible class?

Are you helping rebuild the junior high room so someone else can have space to start a Sunday school class for the deaf?

How about putting some way-paving into action?

Names of people around me in a more prominent ministry	What can I do to help them do their ministry more efficiently?	When will I begin to do it? (date)
1. _____	_____	_____
2. _____	_____	_____
3. _____	_____	_____

You will never know what you can do for others until you begin to look closely and perhaps even ask. How shocked they will be when you ask, "What can I do to help you with your Sunday school class?"

The fourth mark of a way-paver is the ability to focus the glory and honor of the accomplishment upon the Lord. We are not asked to do our good works in a closet. What we do,

even in the area of way-paving, will often be seen by others.
Jesus knew that. He instructed His disciples in Matthew 5:16:
"Let your light shine before men in such a way that they may
see your good works, and glorify your Father who is in heaven."
People will see what we do; yet they should give God the glory.

The following are key factors in assuring that God is given
the glory from your actions.

1. *Keep your eyes heavenward.*

It is the old look-up-into-the-sky-and-others-will-stop-and-
look-up-also ploy, except that you are going to do it spiritually
instead of physically. Keep your own life focused on Jesus, and
those around you will have a tendency to follow your leading.
For instance, when Mrs. McPhail comes up to heap compli-
ments upon you for the beautiful flower arrangement you
placed in the church entry hall, you can immediately reply,
"Isn't the Lord wonderful for making such beautiful and deli-
cately perfect blossoms?"

2. *Explain how your part is only one facet of what God is
doing in the world.*

Do not let anyone (including yourself) view your actions
as having greater value than their actual worth. Whenever
someone you know makes a big point about how much his non-
Christian neighbor enjoyed the Bible study you led last week,
be sure to mention the ministry of hospitality of those who
opened up their home. Mention to him too his own gift of out-
reach in bringing his neighbor to the study in the first place.

3. *Secure a sensitive, loving critic, one who will honestly
evaluate your actions and one who is not afraid to point out
failures.*

Force yourself to really listen to him. We all need a trusted
bubble-popper to keep our pride from swelling.

4. *Collect your praise bouquets and daily present them to
the Lord.*

Corrie Ten Boom is reported to have said that daily she accepts the praise and admiration of others as graciously as possible. Then, each night during her prayers she presents those

affirmations as a beautiful bouquet to the Lord. So must we. He does not mind if we stop to enjoy the fragrance and beauty for a moment as long as we remember to deliver them to Him before they have become faded and wilted.

Being a way-paver is not the easiest task in the world, nor is it a temporary stage that will pass in time. It is an ongoing life-style of hard work, but the rewards are great. Success with a purpose awaits all who are faithful way-pavers.

3

The Pallet Carriers Union

Helping others—that is an important key to greatness. Some folks are so weak spiritually, physically, socially, or mentally that all the way-paving in the world will not help. Such people must literally be picked up and carried to the Lord. That is why we so urgently need more members in the Pallet Carriers Union.

The opening verses of Mark 2 tell the inspiring account of the unnamed founders of that union. Jesus' popularity was on the rise. People everywhere buzzed about His miracles and unusual teachings. That is why such a crowd gathered at Peter's home. Believers and curiosity seekers alike strained to catch a glimpse of the new folk hero, Jesus. Peasants, as well as religious leaders, pushed and shoved their way into and around the small Galilean mud house.

Four in the crowd in particular had more than their own self-interests in mind. They carried their sick, paralyzed friend.

Little is known about the palsied (KJV*), or paralyzed, man, but a general knowledge of history tells us he would be on the lowest rung of the social ladder. Yet, the man was rich in one respect—he had friends who cared. They had carried him from his home through the dusty streets, to bring him to Jesus. Then they found they were crowded out. With great effort they made their way up the outside stairway of Peter's home to the roof, perhaps hoping for an exposed courtyard on top. Such was not the case.

*King James Version.

There they stood, four tired men with a helpless paralytic. Only a few feet separated them from Jesus, yet they were unable to reach Him. What should they do now? Go back home? As they pondered, perhaps one of the men began absent-mindedly scratching at the surface of the hard sun-baked clay roof. Some of it would give way to reveal sticks, branches, and support beams beneath. An idea stirred. Why not remove part of the roof and lower their friend down?

With enthusiasm they scratched, poked, and dug their way through. The noise must have stopped the teaching below. Fear of a cave-in could have panicked the crowd, not to mention the pollution of dirt and dust choking the limited air space. A few shouts of protest (can you imagine Peter taking this quietly?) did not deter the pallet carriers. Soon the hole was big enough to drop the pallet down.

Jesus immediately discerned the situation. He looked at the man and said, "My son, your sins are forgiven."

Sins? Nobody was thinking of sins. All were expecting a healing, of course. The people were intrigued, the scribes outraged. This man assumed power that belonged only to God. (Healing belonged only to God, too, but that could more easily be explained away if need be.)

Jesus dealt with the more serious problem first, but He did not leave the man paralyzed. "Arise, and take up your pallet and walk," He commanded. The man obeyed.

The first ones to meet the paralytic on the street must, undoubtedly, have been the pallet carriers. With jubilant back-slapping and embraces, the little band rejoiced all the way home. They experienced a taste of true greatness (success with a purpose), oblivious to the fact they had initiated the first Pallet Carriers Union.

Suppose you have spent time way-paving. You have helped to remove certain obstacles that kept your friend from coming to Jesus. But a spiritual, physical, social, or mental paralysis might prevent his coming on his own. It is time for you to be a pallet carrier.

There are six important steps to follow in order to be a successful pallet carrier.

1. *Know the needs.* Sometimes we blithely sail through our ministry oblivious to the real hurts and pains of those around us.

Randy is a way-paver. He invited every member of the high school football team to all the church youth group activities. Some came, others refused, and some, like Angelo, seemed caught in indecision. He neither discouraged Randy nor did he ever attend.

After a few months it dawned on Randy that perhaps there were some personal problems holding Angelo back. He took time to get to know him. Angelo lived on the north side of town by the riverbank, in a small home with his parents and six sisters. One day while visiting in Angelo's home, Rosemary, Angelo's sister, asked Randy what church he belonged to. When he replied, she said, "Hey, you must be pretty rich to go to that church. I hear all the big shots go there."

Randy's church was the biggest and most prominent in town, but he had never before considered that a hindrance. He realized for the first time that some in their community viewed it as an impenetrable citadel of affluence. Angelo was socially paralyzed from attending.

2. *Know the source of satisfaction.* The next step is perhaps the hardest. You must be thoroughly convinced that Jesus can completely satisfy the needs of those you bring to Him. That conviction includes not only the faith that Jesus can heal, but faith that He will deal with the real needs of each person, whatever they are.

One day Randy became convinced that Jesus could meet all of Angelo's needs. He showed up Saturday night with a few of his and Angelo's friends and asked Angelo to come with them right then into the city for a Christian music concert. Angelo went.

3. *Begin where they are.* There was no use for the four men to ask the paralytic to meet them at Peter's house. He could

not. They had to go where he was and carry him. They could
have wished he lived closer to the destination. They could have
hoped that he could help them in their attempts, but that was
not possible.

Once in a great while someone might approach you, as the
Philippian jailer approached Paul, and say, "What must I do
to be saved?" What a joy to have such a clear, open opportunity to lead someone to the Lord! Such instances are rare.
Instead, a pallet carrier is prepared to start from the very beginning and carry his friend the whole way.

Armed with a pep talk from his youth director and some
"Five Steps to Conversion" tracts, Randy set out one Thursday
to conquer the world, or at least Angelo. He knew this was the
day. He planned it out. He would bring his lunch and during
the noon break go over to the senior court bench where Angelo
usually sat. There, in the shade of the large sycamore, he would
tell Angelo how to be saved.

But Angelo did not come to school that day. Randy finally
found him about 4:30 P.M. in front of the pool hall with several
of his friends—not exactly an ideal setting.

The surprising thing was, Angelo did want to talk, but not
about spiritual things. He was worried about his sister Rosemary. She was dating Paul Rivera, one of the biggest dope
pushers in town. For two hours Randy listened to Angelo.
No spiritual scalps for the victory belt today. He just began
where Angelo was.

4. *Enlist the help of others.* There is no way for one man to
carry a paralyzed man on a pallet. It would be foolish to try.
That is the way the Lord designed it. He distributed His gifts
among us all and brings us together in communal groups for
their use. No man or woman has ever achieved success with a
purpose, alone. We are a highly dependent race. The person
who sincerely desires success must be willing to bring others
with him. It is the egocentric, carnal Christian who has difficulty sharing his successes. We must admit the limits of our
own ministry and the need of the gifts and talents of others.

At a Sunday night koinonia meeting, Randy shared with his

youth group his growing concern for Angelo. Jim mentioned that he sat next to Angelo in typing. June knew his younger sister Rachael and thought she might help. Angelo soon became the center of prayer and a concerted effort of friendship by the group. Only one difficulty remained.

The cultural barrier was real. Randy knew it should not make a difference, but what is ideal and what is actual are sometimes two different things in this world. That was why someone mentioned Raul. Raul was a member of the Spanish Assembly Church across town and was happy to add Angelo to his prayer list.

That is why it was that Jim, June, Raul, and Randy accompanied Angelo to the concert.

5. *Be persistent.* The crowds and Jesus' seeming inaccessibility did not discourage the determined friends of the paralytic. They were committed to their goal until success had been achieved. Aleksandr Solzhenitsyn calls that doing a thing to the "final inch," pushing on until every possible solution has been tried.

Within Christian work, great programs or missions often fade as quickly as our initial enthusiasm. How sad it is when our half-hearted efforts involve other people.

Recently my hometown newspaper flashed the heartbreaking story of a two-week-old baby found alive, zipped up in a diaper bag, in the bottom of a trash bin. It is difficult to understand why anyone would literally throw away a precious little life. God forgive us for the abandoned pallets we have dumped along our erratic Christian walks. Success takes persistence.

Randy went away to college. Angelo went to work in a factory, but Randy did not give up. An occasional letter, holiday visit, or even a phone call reminded Angelo that Randy still cared.

6. *Be motivated by love.* It might seem impossible to do all of those things for someone and not love them. However, too often love has little to do with our actions.

We can be motivated by duty. That does not mean that you

wait for some sort of tingly sentimental feeling to overwhelm you before you do anything. That is not what love is anyway. Love is caring about another person at least as much as you care about yourself. If that caring can be communicated, then you are on your way to success.

Or we can be motivated by mere success. This whole book emphasizes being successful, but success cannot be our only motive. No one wants to be merely a gold star on your spiritual report card. Success can be a result of pallet carrying, but it is real, live, breathing, hurting, dying, crying people who are lying there on the pallets.

When Randy returned home from college during the Easter break, he went to see Angelo, but he was not home. His sister Rachael explained that Angelo and Raul were down in Mexico on a mission project for Raul's church. She excitedly told how she had led Angelo to the Lord after she became a Christian through Raul's influence. Well, what could he say? The victory belonged to Raul and Rachael. Randy rejoiced that he had completed his mission as an extremely successful pallet carrier.

In order to join the Pallet Carriers Union, you must pay dues. Count the cost; see if you are ready to join.

1. Know the needs. List the persons you know who seem to need to be "carried" to the Lord.

Names: *Needs:*	*Physical*	*Mental*	*Social*	*Spiritual*
a)				
b)				
c)				

2. Know the source of satisfaction. Are you thoroughly convinced that Jesus can meet each of those needs? Write a brief paragraph describing what each of your above friends will be like when Jesus meets their needs.

3. <u>Begin where they are.</u> Do a spiritual inventory. Are they . . .

   a) Non-Christian
- (1) antagonistic
- (2) sympathetic
- (3) complacent

   b) Nominal Christian
- (1) spiritually ignorant
- (2) worldly
- (3) ritualistic

   c) Christian
- (1) rebellious
- (2) lethargic
- (3) enthusiastic

4. <u>Enlist the help of others.</u>

   a) What special spiritual gifts are needed to be of most help?
- (1)
- (2)
- (3)

   b) What mature Christians who demonstrate these spiritual gifts in your fellowship would be willing to help carry the pallet?
- (1)
- (2)
- (3)

I will talk to them about this by ———————.
(date)

5. <u>Be persistent in your actions.</u>

Lord, with Your help, I will be a friend and Pallet Carrier for ————————— until you cure them from their paralysis, meet their deeper needs, or the day You take me home to be with You.

6. <u>Be motivated by love.</u>

Three loving things I am going to do for those I am concerned about by _____.

(date)

a)

b)

c)

4

Get Your Ground Ready to Plant

One of the most obvious ways to measure the success of any ministry is to look at the fruit it produces. The spiritual outcome, the spiritual result, of your actions will give an indication of their value. The fruit of your ministry, both in quantity and quality, is an important source of satisfaction in your service to God. A ministry that never shows positive impact or result is a difficult one to maintain. Like the farmer satisfied with his bountiful harvest in November, so we also are allowed to find contentment in realizing God has used us in a way to bring spiritual benefit to others.

Some caution should be used in evaluating the success of your service. There is the danger of impatience. Often potentially fruitful ministries are prematurely rated as failures merely because of shortsighted and hasty evaluations. Likewise "overnight marvels" should be viewed with some caution until the final test of fruit production can be determined.

Growing up as a California farm boy allowed me the opportunity to learn firsthand a rural philosophy of life. My grandpa once told me, "Stevie, don't ever buy a vineyard in May or a walnut grove in January." It was good advice. The grape vineyards in May are beautiful to behold. Fresh green leaves completely cover the woody, gnarled trunk. Long green runners cascade out from the center of the vine as harmoniously as if placed there by a florist's wise decision. Every vineyard that is still alive at all looks its best in May.

By October the bright, shiny, waxy green leaves have turned hard and dingy looking, coated with dirt, attacked by leafhoppers, covered with sulphur dust to keep the mildew off the fruit. As you lift up those tired looking vines, you will probably be met by a swarm of gnats hiding from the hot glare of the sun; but there tucked away under the foliage will be bunches, and bunches, and bunches of fat, ripe, juicy, tasty grapes. Always buy a vineyard after you have seen it in October.

So also the effectiveness of your ministry must be evaluated only at harvest time, and some ministries demand a long, long growing season. Do not be in too big a hurry to harvest. An unripe grape, as the Scripture says, "sets your teeth on edge."

In the middle of January, a walnut grove is a bleak sight. Without close, knowledgeable examination, you will not be able to tell a dead tree from a live one, for in the midst of winter there are no leaves, no growth, no evidence of a crop. Some ministries seem to go through a long winter, but just wait until the harvest.

One reason many Christians are hesitant in talking about success in their service to the Lord is that they have a great fear of evaluating the effectiveness of their ministry. They have a nagging feeling that they will not like what they find. Sometimes they are right. But whether or not a vine likes it, October does finally arrive. May does not last forever.

Even if we delay our evaluation until Judgment Day, we will still have to face it, sooner or later. First Corinthians 3:13-15 was written for believers: "Each man's work will become evident for the day will show it, because it is to be revealed with fire; and the fire itself will test the quality of each man's work. If any man's work which he has built upon it remains, he shall receive a reward. If any man's work is burned up, he shall suffer loss; but he himself shall be saved, yet so as through fire." The reason for our fear is that we sense that there is more we should be doing to insure success. We should work harder, study more, be more fervent in prayer, and so on. For many of us, our self-diagnosis is probably correct. We often fail to do our part.

What can be done about this rate of failure? At this point we have a great lesson to learn from the parable of the soils

(Mark 4:1-20). Soil preparation is the key to success in farming and is a key to success in ministry as well. It is the hardest, most difficult, most strenuous part of the job, of course, but done correctly it will give us a good foundation for future spiritual harvest.

Before we tackle the parable of the soils, take the following soil test: (Check appropriate response.)

- Whenever I read or hear about Jesus dying on the cross for me,
  - ____ 1. it really does not make much sense, and most of the time I do not pay attention to such words.
  - ____ 2. I remember trying to get saved once; it was OK for a while, but it did not last.
  - ____ 3. I remember that I used to be pretty active in serving God. But I am busy now. Other commitments are crowding my time.
  - ____ 4. I really get all tied up inside. Just imagine—He died for me!

- When the pastor says, "I need two people to call on the convalescent homes every week," I say,
  - ____ 1. "Who, me?"
  - ____ 2. "Oh, sure, that'll be great," and then I call up the next day to back out.
  - ____ 3. "Well, I don't like going into convalescent homes. They're too depressing, and besides, I can't afford to take the time."
  - ____ 4. "Oh, sure! Do you think they'd mind if I went twice a week?"

- When I hear a great sermon,
  - ____ 1. I forget it by lunch.
  - ____ 2. I tell the pastor it was a truly great message and then forget about it by the time I get to work on Monday.
  - ____ 3. I tell the pastor that it was great, remember his his three main points all week, but never take time to do anything about them.

_____ 4. I go out and begin to follow the advice I received. It becomes so much a part of me that I cannot even remember where I learned it.

• When my neighbor was laid off his job last year,
_____ 1. I just figured anybody who gets fired probably is a lazy worker.
_____ 2. I went right over and told him how sorry I was.
_____ 3. I told him I would sincerely like to help him, but then it was vacation time, and I spent every free moment up at the lake with my boat.
_____ 4. I immediately asked my boss at the plant if there were any openings, got my neighbor signed up on the waiting list, and offered to take a day off from work to go with him to the employment agency downtown.

• When an old high school classmate discovered he had cancer,
_____ 1. I forgot all about it until I read his name in the obituaries.
_____ 2. I immediately sent him a humorous get-well card.
_____ 3. I called him on the phone and promised I would stop by the first chance I got, but that chance has not come yet.
_____ 4. I went over to visit, gave him the name of a clinic upstate that helped my brother-in-law, and offered to drive him and his wife up there next week.

Answers 1, 2, 3, and 4 represent the four types of soil in Jesus' parable. Perhaps you discovered that there needs to be some "ground work" in your life before you start worrying about the amount of fruit you are or are not producing.

Jesus was a masterful speaker. By using familiar examples, objects right around where He sat, He could convey to the crowd deep spiritual truth. The parable of the soils is an example of such teaching. His platform was a small fishing boat. He sat or stood in it as it was anchored a short way from the bank. The shoreline was covered with hundreds, maybe thousands, of people. On this occasion it was more important to teach than to touch, so He had purposely separated Himself from the crowd. Even with such a crowd, the fertile farmlands surrounding the Sea of Galilee could be seen. The scene provided Him with just the right object lesson. He described to them four types of soil. Later He reviewed the parable with His disciples and carefully explained the meaning.

The first type of soil was the pathway, the road. The Roman genius for building had brought to Galilee and Judea the idea of well-built stone roadways. Yet most travel was still done on the beaten-down dirt paths of Palestine. Time and toil had so compacted the soil in those areas that it seemed to be impervious to penetration. It was hard enough to bounce a ball on. It could have been swept clean. There is nothing basically wrong with such soil. It bears all the mineral characteristics of the adjoining good farmland. It just literally has the air knocked out of it. Good soil is fluffy. The air pockets are needed both for water storage and for insuring that the roots have some guarded exposure to outside atmosphere. Soil compaction is a key factor to watch in all farming operations.

A person who exhibits the qualities of a path or road is one who has been so compacted, so hardened, that he can no longer receive any spiritual truth. Such truth bounces off the impervious surface like a sunflower seed on a cement driveway. To make sure there is no growth from any attempted planting, Satan will quickly come and remove the truth.

It does not matter much at this point why the soil (or life) was hardened—that is, whose fault it is. Perhaps the hardening is completely the person's own fault. Maybe he has purposely chosen to reject God's help for so long that he can no longer hear it being offered. Or perhaps he is hardened by circumstances that seem to be out of his control. The dangerous thing about a pathway is that once it has begun to be used, everyone will choose the same trail and thus speed its compaction. There is no chance of seed's sprouting, let alone any spiritual growth, until drastic measures are taken.

The second type of soil was the rocky ground. That was the most common type of soil around the hillsides of Judea. Centuries of decomposition and the strong east winds had deposited some soil on the rocky limestone terrain of the hills of Israel. But such soil was often extremely shallow. After a rain, those pockets of moist dirt would certainly provide a home for seed. The seed could sprout and begin to grow. In its early stages such a plant looked as healthy as one growing in the good soil. But time would soon tell the difference. Those same east winds that deposited the soil would now blow off the hot summer desert and dry out the top several inches of ground. The plants in the good, deep, rich soil would merely send their roots deeper into the moist depths, but the plants on the rocky ground, being devoid of depth and ground moisture, could only wither up and die.

Along the foothills of central California where I grew up, there remain testimonies of that principle. During the early part of the century, when farming was first booming in the area, some industrious European immigrants moved in and planted the granite-based hillsides with olive trees. They hoped that the foot or so of dirt covering the rocks plus the rainfall would be sufficient for raising healthy, fruitful trees. To be sure, many of the olive trees began to take root and grow. After one year they looked for the most part as healthy as any others. But time and the blazing San Joaquin Valley sun took its toll. Most of the trees withered and died. All that is left now are a few stunted, misshapen, and unfruitful trees vaguely outlining the rows where someone's fond dream had once stood.

Similar sad reminders of stunted and withered souls plague the landscape of many Christian fellowships and organizations. Jesus said such persons were those who, unlike the pathway person, actually enjoy and receive spiritual truth. In fact, they seem to exhibit much enthusiasm. They learn all the right things to do and say. They are at church every time the doors are opened. They sit in the front row and sing the loudest.

But that was last month. Times have changed; things have gotten rough. The boys at the shop started to ridicule; a good friend stopped coming by to visit; an unexpected illness put the family in financial difficulty; and a promotion at work is denied, because the boss does not like someone who has "got religion." So now the overnight enthusiast has vanished.

Terry was much like the rocky soil of Jesus' parable. He sheepishly entered my office and promptly asked permission to light up a cigarette. I had heard only a little about him from his Christian neighbor. What I had heard was not encouraging. He began to describe his situation—his violent childhood, total rejection by his family and parents, his struggles with the army, the law, and drugs. He told me of his various jobs, wives, and kids. He was depressed to the point of talking about suicide. In tears he asked for my help. I told him of the love of God, of salvation through Christ, of life with meaning, purpose, and satisfaction.

In the now smoke-polluted air of my office, we knelt in prayer as he asked the Lord to come into his life.

Next Sunday Terry and his whole family were in church, with big smiles on their faces. People around him noticed the difference. But before long I realized I had not seen him around for a while. He no longer came to the weekly men's Bible study. When I went to visit, he was never at home. When I called on the phone, he was busy. Finally I got to talk to him. I found him reverted to his earlier life-style of depression. "It's no use," he said. "I tried it and it just didn't last." Before the year was over, he would be back in my office twice more, wanting to be "saved" again, always with the same shallow result.

The third type of soil mentioned by Jesus in the parable was actually good, fluffy, rockless soil. Its problem was that some foreign seed has found its way into the fertile furrows. The grain was planted correctly; there was plenty of water, air, and sunshine; the hot winds did not wilt or wither it; yet it would bear no fruit. Alongside the plants sprouted weeds—weeds that robbed the grain of its proper share of moisture, weeds whose leaves blocked the grain from the needed sunlight. The

plant was so busy trying merely to stay alive among the competition of the weeds that it remained fruitless.

Jesus reminded his followers that some people are that way.
They have a lot of natural potential for much greatness, success
with a purpose, but it is wasted on weeds rather than plants.
The weeds, Jesus said, were (1) the worries of the world,
(2) the deceitfulness of riches, and (3) the desire for things.

• The worries of the world include:
  1. health, age, fear of death, hunger, cancer, disease, and
     so forth
  2. personal peace, wanting to be left alone, not bothered
     by others; anything to make life easier
  3. social acceptance, personal need to be "one of the
     boys," wanting others' approval no matter what it takes
     to achieve it

The worries of the world become possessive. They occupy
one's thoughts and energies. The person loses sight of his own
spiritual progress and is swallowed up into impotency by the
burden of worldly concerns.

• The deceitfulness of riches includes:
  1. bill-paying blues—end-of-the-month conflict of who
     gets the money
  2. happiness for sale the still popular belief that material
     goods produce the happy life
  3. the "American dream"—if you are rich you must be
     successful

• The desire for things includes:
  1. charge accounts—where luxuries become necessities
  2. dissatisfaction—the insatiable urge to get more
  3. one-upmanship—whoever possesses the most "things"
     must be the greater person

Weeds are very deceptive. They start as small, green, harm-
less little leaves that really do not hurt anything. Yet they grow

at an alarming rate and prove themselves extremely difficult to eradicate. Take, for instance, the morning glory.

In some parts of our country, the morning glory is a garden flower. But in central California the wild morning glory is a troublesome pest and a destroyer. Its rapid, vinelike growth quickly entangles and strangles every crop it comes in contact with. It is a pest to trees, stalks, vines, and vegetable plants alike. Simple hoeing only spreads its roots, and each begins to grow anew. Few chemicals can really harm it. It is best taken care of by digging it out by the roots and burning it, before the tiny seeds are allowed to replant themselves in the rich farm soil. A lazy farmer who refuses to do so will soon have his entire acreage overrun with morning glories.

Likewise, the worries of the world, the deceitfulness of riches, and the desire for things fill up the time and effort of life, so entangling a man's thoughts, attitudes, and actions that any fleeting effort at spiritual success is completely choked out.

The fourth type of soil Jesus mentioned was the good soil. Good soil is a joy to behold. My old farm boy instincts get excited as I run that dark, moist, crumbling, fresh soil between my fingers. It is not sticky like clay; it is not grainy like sand. I can feel its richness on my bare feet and almost smell its vitality.

The spiritual life, like that good soil, has three positive qualities. First, it hears the word—that is, it perceives spiritual truth. That truth might come from hearing the Word preached or taught. Perhaps it comes from the private reading of Scripture. Or it might be through the direct work of the Holy Spirit in a life. Whatever the circumstances, there is exposure to God's truth.

Unlike some of the other soils, the good soil not only hears but also accepts spiritual truth. That does not mean merely storing up facts in a memory bank, but rather, really letting it sink in, fully understanding the matter.

The third quality of good soil is that it acts upon what it receives. The fruit-bearing spiritual life is not content to hear and receive; it wants to change and be changed. God reveals truth for a purpose. If it is not used, it soon becomes as rancid as leftover manna.

One of the difficulties in applying the parable about the soils is the idea that the whole "field" has only one type of soil. That is seldom true in farming or true in our lives. The same small orchard might contain an abandoned cow trail of tightly packed dirt, a streak of old river bed with many rocks, a patch of morning glories or Johnson grass, and much good soil. Each of us desiring to serve the Lord has some areas of hardness to new truth, some shallowness of commitment, some overgrowth of worldly worries, and, it is hoped, some real spiritual depth.

The amount of crop harvested will depend to some degree on how much work you did to prepare the soil. You will never be able to sit back and wait in peace for the harvest until you are convinced that you have done all you can yourself. Therefore, you are going to need to get your ground ready to plant. The following steps will help you to put this into action.

1. *Wait for the early rain!* What a strange statement. I have just told you to get busy, and now I tell you to wait. The reason is this: old ground (whether pathway, rocky, weedy, or good) is best worked up for next year's crop only *after* the first fall rains have softened it up. Spiritual success comes about only when God has first initiated the action. Prayer is the best spiritual field softener I know of—down-on-your-knees, heart-searching, soul-yielding prayer. As you pray, God will begin to show you the hard pathways in your life—the rocks, the thorns, and the weeds. Then and only then will you be ready to proceed. Perhaps you need to make a covenant with yourself that goes something like this:

Because I desire healthy spiritual growth and much spiritual fruit in my life, I will spend _____ minutes per day in prayer that I might have God's leading in this matter.

2. *Turn over the fallow ground.* Fallow ground is good soil that has been left unseeded. It becomes hard and compacted when not in use. It must be plowed, turned over. Even the most crusted roadways can be restored to good farm ground with the proper tools and timing. Many of us have a certain

hardness in our hearts in some area of spiritual growth. It is usually the old, don't-confuse-me-with-the-facts-I've-already-made-up-my-mind routine.

At one point in my spiritual pilgrimage, I decided that gospel tracts were a shallow, gimmicky, inefficient, and pushy way to spread Christianity. There was no reason to tell me about how many people were getting saved through them; I had already made up by mind. Then, in a time of prayerful soul searching about what needed to be done to increase my evangelism effectiveness, the Lord brought to mind this bit of stubborn, hard pathway in my life. Old habits of thought were hard to turn over, but with the right spiritual rain it turned out to be fruitful ground.

3. *Remove the rocks in your field.* One of the hardest jobs on the farm was to walk behind the tractor, tossing rocks into the trailer all day long. The rock needed to be removed before any planting could be done. Our own pride and ego are often the biggest boulders in our fields. They hold us back with shallow commitment, making us hesitate to completely give ourselves to the Lord's work. When such rocks remain, our spiritual fields will look like a half-finished, wilted, abandoned farm. Use the following chart to analyze your present ministry activities.

1. List the three most important projects you are currently planning to do for the Lord.	2. Carefully list everything you believe is necessary to achieve maximum success in these areas.	3. Which of these (#2) are you failing to give wholehearted effort to?	4. Do any of these projects already look half-finished, wilted, abandoned?
a.			
b.			
c.			

4. *Pull out the weeds before you plant the seeds.* Weeds grow fast; use that to your advantage. Often after the first rain, the

field is plowed and left to sit for a while. During that time the weeds start their growth. That happens to be the best time to go out and dig them up. For us on the farm it meant digging down carefully to make sure we got all roots and stuffing them into a gunny sack—then making sure they were all burned up to ensure no further propagation. It is futile and even lazy to merely chop off those kinds of weeds; they must be dug out.

The worries of the world, the deceitfulness of riches, the desire for things must all be dealt with very carefully. If you want to harvest a big spiritual crop, then the covetousness, pettiness, lust for money, and worldly goals must be dug up by the roots and completely destroyed.

Sin chokes every ministry. Your effectiveness is automatically reduced until you deal clearly with those matters. You must learn to identify and eradicate the weeds of sin. Here are a few of the most common ones.

- *fearus catastrophitis* a fast growing, doomsday, drab-colored vine that entwines itself around every living thing. It produces a hypnotic effect when gazed upon for any length of time.

- *plentius moneyugus* a green, silver, or gold broadleaf plant with brightly colored seed pods. The seeds when eaten cause insatiable addiction among humans.

- *covetous climber* (common name: GimmeGimme plant) a plant with beautiful, multicolored flowers, which tend to grow in the opposite direction from humans but can be reached by much hard work. However, they immediately wilt when plucked.

5. *Plant the seeds.* You have done the preliminary work; now plant the seeds in the loose, moist earth. With the Lord's help you have turned over old pathways, you have thrown out the rocks and pulled out the weeds. Do not stop now; you have finished the hardest part. Begin to sow those seeds. Begin those ministries you would like to be involved in. Use all those

gifts and talents that the Lord has given you. Plant the "crops" you are good at raising, but try a little something new also. Do not hold back. It will mean getting your hands dirty, but do not leave any part of your spiritual field unplanted. Remember a nice, clean, freshly plowed field that is not used will turn into a hard, weedy, and shallow wasteland in a very short time.

6. *Wait for the spring rains.* Your job was to clear the land, turn over the soil, and plant the seed. God brings the rain and the sunshine, and it is up to the seed itself to sprout and grow. The seed, God's Word, is guaranteed. Likewise, the rain and the sun are in God's total control. No matter how self-sufficient we think we have become, only God can bring growth, maturity, and harvest.

The amount of spiritual greatness—success with a purpose— you achieve will depend upon the kind of soil you begin with. Therefore, you must begin to get your ground ready to plant.

5

Planning Your Future Success

Jesus wanted His followers to taste success for themselves. He was not content for them to merely trail along after Him, experiencing ministry from a distance. At the proper time He opened wide the door to the world and pushed them out on their own. It was God's plan all along to entrust His work to the hands of ordinary people. It was Jesus' role to see that some were ready to begin that ministry when He left this world. How did He carry out such a training assignment?

In Mark 3:13-18 and the parallel passage in Luke 6:12-19, we find the procedure that Jesus used in the process of discipleship training. Jesus began by spending an entire night in prayer (Luke 6:12).

How phenomenal it seems to us that Jesus should ever need to spend an entire night praying. What a dramatic example that is for us!

Has there ever been anything important enough in your life to spend an entire night praying about it? Surely there has. However, did you actually do it?

Remember when your loved one was in the intensive care unit of the hospital? Or when you needed to decide whether or not to take that new job and move to a new community? How about when your sister had marital problems (or maybe it was you)? Or perhaps it was your burden that the Sunday school should grow? In any case, most of us at one time or another have inwardly felt the necessity for intense prayer. In Romans 15:30 Paul calls it "striving" in prayer.

All attempts at success might as well be discarded until you are seriously ready to spend an ample amount of time at the business of praying. Jesus' personal example is all too plain at this point.

"What do I say? What do I do?"

"All night long? I'll run out of things to say or fall asleep by 10:00 P.M."

Perhaps the following guide will be helpful.

Situation: You have been asked by your pastor to be the director of your church's mid-week youth program. You have agreed to pray about it. You explain to your family why it is you will need to spend all Friday night up and around the house.

Friday Night Schedule:

10:00 Family goes to bed. You begin your prayer night.

10:00-11:00 This hour you will spend concentrating solely on your heavenly Father.

- Read Bible passages about the greatness and glory of God (such as Genesis 1-2; Exodus 3-4; Deuteronomy 4-6; Job 38-42; Psalms 139-150; Isaiah 40-55; etc.). Spend about thirty minutes.
- Read through or sing quietly several hymns that focus your attention on God's greatness (for example, "A Mighty Fortress," "O God, Our Help in Ages Past," "Praise to the Lord, the Almighty," "How Great Thou Art," "Because He Lives," etc.). Spend about ten minutes.
- Spend the next twenty minutes in prayer, expressing your own feelings about God's majesty and greatness. If you run out of anything to say, quietly wait for Him to reveal Himself to you.

11:00-12:00 Spend this time thinking about yourself.

- Jot down the five most crucial decisions you have ever made, the most exciting thing that has happened in the past year, the ten people you are most thankful to the Lord for bringing into your life. Consider your own conversion and all that God has done for you. About thirty minutes.
- Spend twenty minutes in prayer, thanking God for all He has done for you in the past, for every good gift, friend, and blessing He has brought your way.

- Read or sing quietly your three favorite hymns or choruses. About ten minutes.

12:00-12:30 Have a cup of chocolate, soup, coffee, or tea. Step out into your backyard and gaze at the expanse of stars, observe the stillness of the night, or just enjoy the freshness of the air. Consider the intricacies of God's creation around you.

12:30-1:30 Spend this time thinking about Jesus.
- Consider His life and ministry. Read several chapters out of your favorite gospel and Colossians 1, Philippians 2, Hebrews 1. About thirty minutes.
- Read through or sing quietly several songs about Jesus (Such as "Fairest Lord Jesus," "O for a Thousand Tongues to Sing," "The Old Rugged Cross," "He Keeps Me Singing," "The King Is Coming," etc.). Use about ten minutes.
- Review in your mind, with a thankful heart, the events in the life of our Lord. Consider what His life and death have meant for you personally. Spend twenty minutes in prayer and adoration.

1:30-2:30 Now you can get down to the actual decision at hand.
- Read carefully and thoughtfully the book of Ephesians. Twenty minutes.
- Write down everything you know about the job of mid-week youth program director. What will you be doing? How much time will you need to give? Who will you be working with? What impact will this have on your family? Twenty minutes.
- Pray for twenty minutes specifically about this position. Ask God to show you any more aspects of this ministry that you might be overlooking. As He reveals something to you, write it down, then continue praying.

2:30-3:00 Give yourself another soup, coffee, or tea break, but do not let yourself be distracted from your immediate task. Forget about the newspaper, business deals, a messy house.

Step outside again and just thank God for agreeing to spend the night listening to you.

3:00-4:00   Examine the problems.

- Read the first five chapters of Acts. Get the flavor for ministry in the early church. Twenty minutes.
- List every reason that pops into your head why you should *not* accept this position. Ten minutes.
- Review this list and place each reason in order of importance. Therefore, number one is your most serious objection. Ten minutes.
- Take this list to the Lord in prayer. Present each reason to Him. Let Him convict you of which reasons should be dropped or changed in priority or perhaps what new reason should be added. About twenty minutes.

4:00-5:00   Take a look at the positive side.

- Read 1 and 2 Timothy. Notice Paul's continual encouragement of Timothy's ministry. Twenty minutes.
- Take ten minutes to list every reason you can think of that you should accept this position.
- Use another ten minutes and put this list in order of priority.
- Take this list to the Lord in prayer and listen to Him as He emphasizes, deletes, or adds reasons to your list. About twenty minutes.

5:00-6:00   Time for decision.

- Read James 1. Ask God's wisdom in making your decision. Five minutes.
- Review both of the revised lists you now have. On the basis of your knowledge of God, your knowledge of your own gifts, and your knowledge of His will for your life, make a temporary decision either to accept or decline the position. About ten to twenty minutes.
- Write out your decision and list the three top reasons to support it. Five minutes.
- Take this decision to the Lord. Ask Him either to confirm

it or reject it. Thank Him for His gracious answer. Ten minutes.

- Sing quietly or read through several of your favorite praise songs ("Alleluia," "Amazing Grace," "To God Be the Glory," etc.). Ten minutes.
- Spend some time just visiting with the Lord. Do not worry about your decision. Express gratitude to Him and let Him prompt your heart. Twenty minutes.

6:00-Noon Go to bed and sleep (which, of course, should be previously arranged with your family).

Noon Get up. Read your decision to your family. Ask their prayers. Call your pastor and give him your decision, stating your reasons.

The next step Jesus took to insure the success of His ministry on earth was actually to select those few whom He would disciple and train. He did not post an "Apostles Sign-Up List" on the bulletin board. He did not put a notice in the weekly worship bulletin. He did not even call a congregational meeting and ask for a general election. Jesus appointed the twelve.

The above methods that Jesus bypassed might be effective for some events. You can have sign-ups for church potlucks or volleyball teams. But, sometimes the ministry project is so crucial you must have exactly the right person on the job; just anybody will not always do. A careful combining of the right gifts, talents, and ministries is extremely important.

When we seek out and select certain individuals, there is always the possibility that someone will be left behind who possibly wanted the job. Surely there were some whom Jesus "left behind" also. Mark 3:13 points out that Jesus removed Himself from the general crowd, then called out the twelve. Years later when the apostolic band believed they should select another member to replace Judas, they listed as a qualification one who had "accompanied us all the time that the Lord Jesus went in and out among us—beginning with the baptism of John" (Acts 1:21-22).

Jesus did not choose His disciples at random, either. We have two clues that He knew exactly what He was doing. First, we are told that He "summoned those whom He Himself wanted" (v. 13). Second, notice how well He knew those men. To several, He assigned familiar nicknames. Simon became Peter, "the rock." James and John became Boanerges, "sons of thunder." Jesus well knew Peter's stubbornness and also James's and John's quick tempers.

The twelve apostles did not at first glance possess the tremendous leadership qualities that we would associate with the success of any great movement. They might not have received the "Most Likely to Succeed" awards from the Greater Galilean Chamber of Commerce. Here is the advantage of knowing people well. Jesus knew their potential when properly motivated and empowered by the Holy Spirit. Even though it might look to the contrary (such as on the night of His betrayal), Jesus made no mistakes in selecting the twelve.

The success of many projects we are involved in often depends upon the ability of other people to carry out their part of the task. How can we be assured they will follow through? We are not always in a position to select our co-workers. We are often the selectees, not the selector. But, the time could come when it is your responsibility to choose workers. You will want to select just the right people. Perhaps the following six steps will be helpful.

1. Spend time in prayer.

2. Write a one paragraph job description of what the person(s) will be doing.

3. List the gifts, talents, and ministries needed for the success of this job.

    a)   *d*)

    b)   *e*)

    c)   *f*)

4. Which people most closely qualify, regardless of their current involvement in other areas?

    a)

    b)

    c)

    d)

Now, list in order of priority:

    #1 choice ————————————

    #2 choice ————————————

    #3 choice ————————————

    #4 choice ————————————

5. Ask God if there is any reason why you should not ask the person who is your first choice. Listen to Him. Wait several days, then ask Him again.

6. Talk to your first choice. Do not be apologetic. Simply share your enthusiasm for the ministry you are proposing.

    a) Show him the job description.
    b) Show him a list of gifts, talents, and ministries needed for the job.
    c) Tell him why you think he is the very best for the job.
    d) Rejoice when he accepts.
    e) Understand if he refuses. At this point proceed with your second choice. Perhaps the Lord has a different preference order than you do.

"But, all of this takes so much time, work, and energy," you say.

Right. But remember, this book is not written for those who are satisfied with a mediocre Christian life-style. This is written for those who want the Lord to use every ability He has given them. There is a price to pay for success.

After Jesus completed the first two steps (prayer and appointment), He then explained the third—assignment of ministry. It is very clear why Jesus called those twelve. They were to:

1. *Be with Jesus.* That is not to be underestimated. Jesus knew He could not effectively train the multitudes (given the human limits that He voluntarily accepted). So, the twelve were selected to share the intimacies of life with the Master.

2. *Go out and preach.* You might call that "student training." The bulk of the disciples' preaching would come after Jesus was gone; now was the time to learn.

3. *Have power over Satan.* The training and assignment were very important, but the power to carry out their mission was extremely necessary. Our successes as Christians must be at Satan's expense. We must learn spiritual warfare.

How do those steps apply to your own situation? Suppose you have prayerfully accepted a challenging task. You have carefully selected those who will work with you.

First, your co-workers need an opportunity to watch your example. That goes for filing library cards or making evangelistic house calls. They are to be with you. That makes you vulnerable too, for they will also get to know you as a person.

Second, they need a chance to do it on their own. Easy in theory, that is sometimes the most difficult step in practice.

Third, you must sufficiently prepare them to meet and overcome the attacks of Satan. For the apostles this meant knowing how to cast out demons. That might not be the exact kind of power your co-worker will need. However, he will need to know that the power that is within him is greater than the power in this world (1 John 4:4). Satan can use every tool he has, from boredom to depression to threat of bodily harm.

If such talk about the power of the Holy Spirit in your life seems strange to your ears, you are due for a review of the work of the third Person of the Trinity. Books that will help you and your co-workers discover (or rediscover) the power of a Spirit-filled life are: *The Spirit-filled Life* (Campus Crusade for Christ International, Arrowhead Springs, San Bernardino, CA 92403); Charles C. Ryrie, *The Holy Spirit* (Chicago: Moody, 1973); John Stott, *The Baptism and Fullness of the Holy Spirit* (Downer's Grove, Ill.: InterVarsity, 1964); and John F. Walvoord, *The Holy Spirit at Work Today* (Chicago: Moody, 1973).

Some Christians have serious concerns about planning. It sounds unbiblical, so they say, to "plan" one's ministry. Scripture references are pulled out to support that. Let us look at those passages.

> Come now, you who say, 'Today or tomorrow, we shall go to such and such a city, and spend a year there and engage in business and make a profit.' Yet you do not know what your life will be like tomorrow. You are just a vapor that appears for a little while and then vanishes away. Instead, you ought to say, 'If the Lord wills, we shall live and also do this or that' (James 4:13-15).

That passage clearly points out one of the dangers of planning—that is, forgetting that all plans are subject to God's continuing approval and revision. It does not say we should not plan. In fact, it says the opposite. First we give God his proper place. Then we go ahead and carry out our plans.

Another often quoted verse: "Therefore do not be anxious for tomorrow; for tomorrow will care for itself. Each day has enough trouble of its own" (Matthew 6:34). Is Jesus saying not to worry about making plans for tomorrow because everything will work out all right? No. Go back and read all of Matthew 6:25-34. He is specifically talking about what you are going to eat or drink tomorrow. God will provide. And He is not suggesting we buy groceries or clothing to last only one day. He is speaking of needless anxiety about the material things of this world.

Many a poor lesson or sermon has been based on a faulty interpretation of Matthew 10:19: "But when they deliver you up, do not become anxious about how or what you will speak; for it shall be given you in that hour what you are to speak."

Some say you should not plan a lesson or sermon. Just wait until the time comes and suddenly it will all come to you. Jesus was speaking about the future persecution, suffering, and imprisonment His disciples would face for His name's sake. In that situation (i.e., standing before tribunals for the gospel's sake), they would be given the words needed. In the meantime we should plan and prepare to our utmost in order to present the very best ministry possible.

Three of the most effective planners in Scripture are Moses, Paul, and Jesus. Exodus 18 shows Moses desperately needing the advice on planning he received from his father-in-law, Jethro. Romans 1:1-15; 15:22-33 shows how Paul planned to carry out his missionary journey to Spain. Jesus often refused to go along with the crowd (Mark 1:35-39; John 2:4; 6:15; 7:6, 8, 30; 8:20) because doing so did not fit into His plans. His statement was often, "My hour has not yet come." Jesus had a plan of ministry; everything had its "right time."

The chance of your finding success with a purpose without thoughtful, prayerful planning is extremely remote. Yet with Christ-inspired plans, you can look for and enjoy real spiritual success. The following Spiritual Planner, with searching answers on your part, could insure a good start on any project.

Spiritual Planner

    1. Who will benefit from this action?

2. What must happen before I can do my part?

3. What action(s) will be required from me?

4. Who will help determine if I have succeeded?

5. What result do I want from this ministry?

6

People You Meet on the Path to Success

What a break! For weeks and weeks Jesus had preached the Kingdom of God throughout Galilee and exhibited amazing power over Satan. The common people rejoiced. Many in high places had appeared not to be overly impressed with the carpenter from Nazareth. Now the situation was changing.

A synagogue official approached Jesus for help (Mark 5:21-43). This man was not a priest or rabbi, but he oversaw the synagogue building and arrangements for all services. "Synagogue official" was a highly prized title held by only a few distinguished members. With much humility the official threw himself down at Jesus' feet and begged Him to come and heal his daughter.

The disciples must have been quite excited. At last, Jesus' ministry was getting the exposure it needed. The leaders were coming around. Perhaps soon there would be official acceptance of Jesus. Of course, Jesus knew better. But He did not hesitate to agree to go with Jairus. And the swarms of people followed, packed in tightly all around them.

In that crowd was an unnamed lady who would be known throughout history as "the woman with a hemorrhage." She had in mind a miracle healing of her own. She pushed and jostled her way through the people in order to touch Jesus. At the dramatic moment when her hand felt the hem of His cloak, two exciting things happened.

Instant healing flooded the woman's body, and Jesus stopped the whole procession to ask, "Who touched Me?"

The disciples, possibly irritated for any delay in this important mission to Jairus's house, were almost indignant. "What do You mean, 'Who touched Me'? The whole crowd is touching You. So what?"

As Jesus looked at her, the woman stumbled through the now still crowd with fear and trembling and fell down before Him. And even though an important man's little daughter was sick to the point of death, Jesus took time to listen to the woman's life story. We only get a condensed version, but we do know:

- she had gone to many doctors
- she had gone through many treatments
- she spent all her money
- nothing had given her relief
- in the past months she had been getting worse
- she had heard of Jesus' healing ministry
- she believed He could help her

Anyone relating such a story certainly would have taken some time to do it. It must have disturbed the disciples greatly. Their worst fears came true when Jairus's friends approached to report that it was too late; his daughter was dead. We know, of course, that Jesus later raised her to life. But, the important thing here is to note Jesus' sensitivity to the needs of others.

If Jesus had hurried on His way to the official's house without questioning the woman, would she have been any less healed? I think not. Yet, He stopped and listened. It is in that pause that we learn a principle of success.

To Jesus, all people, common people, famous people, old people, young people, were important. He realized the lady with the hemorrhage had more than just physical needs. Jesus cared enough to lay aside His immediate plans for a time and listen.

Careful planning should *never* prevent you from paying close attention to the needs of individual people. Excellent planning, without personal and spiritual sensitivity, leads to a computerized, mechanical religion.

I like to get to church very early on Sunday mornings for a quiet time of private devotions and final preparations for the morning's classes and worship. The time is carefully blocked into my weekly schedule. It is one of my prime times with the Lord.

About six o'clock one morning I heard what sounded like a knock at my office window. At first I thought it was just the east wind blowing against a shrub. As it persisted, I stopped what I believed was very important work on my sermon and entered the dimly lit church courtyard to discover Diane.

Diane was a stranger to me. She told me she was waiting for a bus home. The depot was just a block away and she was getting cold, so she went for a walk and saw my light. She wondered if I had a cup of coffee to share.

I am ashamed to admit it, but that did not seem like a reasonable request to me at the time. After all, I was working on my sermon. I had many sheep to feed, and the Lord required my very best preparation. Besides, this was scheduled time. All of that rushed through my mind as I stood at the doorway and told the young lady I did not think we had any coffee, but maybe she could get some downtown.

As I walked back to my office I tried to justify my action. Normally I make coffee, but that morning I had not got around to it. Any other morning it would have been ready to share. Before I closed the door I thought, *Who do I think I am to leave that girl out in the cold?*

Sheepishly I called out to her and invited her back. I took time to make coffee and heard her story. Since her bus was going to arrive soon, I could offer little more than the hot drink, use of the ladies' room, and a few dollars for something to eat on the way home. I glanced at the clock when she left: 6:50 A.M. The whole process had taken fifty minutes, fifty minutes that I almost did not give. I seriously doubt that the morning's sermon was adversely affected. I shudder to think of how many other Dianes I have overlooked in striving to keep to schedules.

Planning is essential for ministry—but then, so is flexibility.

All plans are subject to the Lord's interruptions. In fact, I believe that flexibility can be scheduled into your day. Take a look at the following steps.

1. *Plan to go somewhere or do something.* A mighty oak is flexible enough to grow around and over a solid rock, but it is steadily growing in its pattern. Obviously, if you are not going anywhere, you need not think about being flexible. Many Christians have no idea in what direction the Lord is leading them. They have no idea what they are aiming for—one year, five years, ten years from now. Do you?

Suppose, for instance, you determine that in five years you should be using your spiritual gifts by teaching an adult class at church. In the meantime, how do you prepare? Suppose you decide to enroll in night school courses at a local Bible school. Suppose you also decide to start a more systematic study of Scripture, with the thought that you might be teaching this material some day. In addition, you commit yourself to reading all the background books you can find. Finally, you decide to attend a Sunday school teacher's training convention in your state. Now you have some direction, some goals. You are going somewhere.

At this point you must translate all of this into your daily activity. This morning you will start that systematic study. At your noon break you plan to write a letter of inquiry to the Bible school. After work you plan to stop by the church library and check out a few background books. You will also pick up a registration form for the convention. Now you have translated your five-year goal into a day-sized piece.

2. *Recognize each conversation this day as a God-appointed encounter.* Even though you have your day carefully planned, someone might come along who could force you to revise it. Your daily goals, as mentioned above, are of a spiritual nature, but no goals stand beyond the limit of God's redirection.

People are important. The lady with the hemorrhage was just as important to Jesus as was Jairus's daughter. Diane, the girl at my window, is just as important to the Lord as each individual in the congregation I serve. The bank teller, the lady at the coffee shop, and the old man standing at the bus stop are just as important as the registrar at the Bible school, the church secretary, and the dynamic speaker at the convention.

3. *Always keep in mind which activities could be eliminated or postponed, if necessary.* Take time with this, as we are often fooled as to what is truly important. Suppose your day looks like this:

6:00- 7:00	Begin systematic study of Bible
7:00- 8:00	Clean up, have breakfast, go to work
8:00-12:00	Work
12:00- 1:00	Lunch and write letters
1:00- 5:00	Work
5:00- 6:30	Stop by church office and library
6:30- 7:30	Dinner with family
7:30- 9:00	PTA meeting at junior high
9:00-10:30	Read new book on biblical backgrounds
10:30	Bed

Which of those are most easily set aside in case God brings someone unexpectedly into your life today? Certainly the interruption would need to be very drastic to be worthy of your missing work. Your job is your responsible means of supporting your family or meeting your commitments to those employers and employees who count on you. On the other hand, such things as letters, a trip to the library, and independent study could be postponed to another day, if necessary.

And what about the PTA meeting? How important is it? What kind of interruption would be legitimate? If your son has a solo in the band recital, which is part of the program that night, that would certainly make it more important. On the other hand, perhaps you could spend your noon hour tomorrow at the county hospital where the junior high band will be doing the same program. If the need is great, perhaps the PTA meeting is flexible.

What about the meals? That's right, the meals. Is it critical that you not miss any meals? A few people do have health problems that require certain eating habits, but most of us could do without once in a while. Perhaps the urgent needs of a fellow worker are more important than your lunch.

Once you have in mind which items in your tentative schedule are flexible, then you have an idea how to adjust to unforeseen encounters.

4. *Whenever you meet a person, look for and listen for verbal and nonverbal signs of deeper needs.* Many people can be read like a book, providing we take time to learn the language. Very few words need be spoken, yet you can know just how your spouse is feeling. A certain amount of this kind of sensitivity can be developed toward others.

Slow down long enough to give each person a chance to mention something meaningful. One way to do this is to begin to set your own conversation on a spiritual level. That often provides others an "in" to something meaningful. For instance, "Nice weather we're having," could be "The Lord sure created a beautiful day today, didn't He?"

Instead of answering, "Fine," when someone asks, "How are you?" you could say, "Well, I had the beginnings of a cold last week, but the Lord gave me the strength I needed to make it through vacation Bible school." That just might open up the conversation to a health need of your friend, which might lead to your offering encouragement or instruction from the Scriptures. Learn to read not only his conversation, though, but tone, attitudes, eyes, and heart.

5. *Develop methods of building and strengthening the faith of others.* One way to do this is to develop instant prayer habits. On the way out of church a fellow choir member mentions in passing, "Hey, pray for me. I've got to take some medical tests tomorrow." Stop him right on the spot and pray for him.

When the repairman comments on your statement about having the Lord's strength for Bible school last week, saying he wished he had some extra strength for all the hard work he has lined up for that day, ask him if you can pray for him, and do it.

When your neighbor calls to tell you again of the trouble

Billy is having in junior high, ask her if you can pray with her right there on the phone.

Another way to build up others is to develop a praise attitude toward life. Look for ways to accent the positive. A thankful optimist can overcame a dozen gloomy pessimists. Look for the beauty, the joy, the good things in every situation, in every person. Paul gave not mere poetic rhetoric, but practical instruction for living when he said, "Finally, brethren, whatever is true, whatever is honorable, whatever is right, whatever is pure, whatever is lovely, whatever is of good repute, if there is any excellence and if anything worthy of praise, let your mind dwell on these things" (Philippians 4:8).

Of course, we must not fail to really hear the hurts and pains and struggles that others go through and feel those things with them. We can help our friends see the whole of life, keeping a proper balance and perspective before God. Paul found that the Lord was so great, His love for us so deep, that he could truly rejoice at all times. Such an attitude will be a wonderful strength to the people around us.

Finally, we can build and strengthen the faith of others by becoming their personal promoters. Our society leans to the concept that we advance in life by pulling others down. Conversations often center on cutting remarks about others.

Jesus had the ability to make others feel accepted and important. Think of Zacchaeus (Luke 19), the woman caught in adultery (John 8), the woman at the well (John 4), or Nathanael (John 1). Jesus' trademark was taking sincere people who had little to offer the world in terms of prestige and making them feel important. We can do no less.

6. *Allow God to surprise you.* Just when you think your whole schedule is botched because you took time for someone else, the Lord does some wonderful work to allow you to complete your tasks as well.

Finding an hour to drive to a neighboring city and pick up some books was going to be a difficult task for me during a recent busy week. Yet it had to be done. The second graders must have their promotion Bibles. When the appointed time to go arrived, Sherry was in my office, in tears, telling me of her pregnant teenage daughter. Here was real human need at the deepest level. By the time we were through the store was closed. No Bibles.

But about six o'clock that evening a woman rang our doorbell. One of the employees of the bookstore lived only a block away from us and had decided to deliver my order on her way home. The old schedule, with surprise help from the Lord, was held intact.

One secret to success: Keep planning. Keep looking for those divine interruptions. Keep expecting those surprise provisions.

7

Ministry Partners

There are some things a person just cannot do alone. It is almost impossible, all by yourself, to:

- get something out of your eye
- hold an enlightening conversation
- complain
- see if your shirt matches your socks
- tell a joke
- bandage a wound on your back
- move a heavy sofa
- play tennis

Likewise, in the spiritual realm there are many things we cannot do alone, such as

- see our own sin clearly
- discuss spiritual truths
- express our hurts and griefs
- examine our doctrine
- share our joy
- battle it out with Satan
- comfort our own broken hearts
- remove barriers
- see beyond our narrowness

One of the hardest things for any Christian to do by himself is to successfully complete a ministry. In God's wisdom, He rarely assigns a ministry that will be completely independent of others. Jesus is the only one who conceivably could have. But certainly His followers could not and did not.

Even the apostle Paul always travelled in the company of others. It was Barnabas and Paul who left Antioch on that first missionary journey. Their second time out, Paul and Silas went one way, Barnabas and John Mark went another.

Jesus knew that would be the best way. In Mark 6:7, He sent the disciples out in pairs. In Luke 10:1 when He sent out the seventy, they went two by two. Partnership is certainly a key to true spiritual greatness.

There are five reasons you need to have a ministry partner.

1. *The task you are trying to accomplish may be much larger than any one person can handle.* Our Lord has many tasks to be completed before He returns. Most of those are exciting undertakings that will change many lives. Very few can be completed by any one person.

In Acts 11 we learn that the apostles heard of a new, fast growing church in Antioch. They sent Barnabas to check it out. When he arrived he found a vital group of fairly new believers who were preaching the Lord Jesus. Barnabas rejoiced, but also recognized their need for solid, deep teaching. He was wise enough to know that he could not handle the teaching task alone.

He left for Tarsus to find Paul and brought him back. Together they trained several other leaders, so that the church soon had five pastors (Acts 13).

2. *No one person is completely gifted in all areas.* Paul makes clear in 1 Corinthians 12 that there are varieties of gifts, varieties of ministries, and varieties of effects. "But to each one is given the manifestation of the Spirit for the common good" (v. 7).

Philip, the evangelist, was one of the first to travel into Samaria with the gospel. Acts 8 tells of his ministry. As he preached, many turned to the living God and gave up their pagan ways. Philip apparently had a deficiency in his ministry in the area of teaching about the filling and power of the Holy Spirit; but that problem was soon remedied. Peter and John arrived on the scene and completed what was lacking in Philip's ministry. Philip, Peter, and John ministering together insured a solid base for the Samaritan church.

There are, indeed, "superstars" in the Christian ministry, but even renowned evangelists would be the first to say that their ministries would be impossible without ministry partners. An evangelistic crusade is the culmination of weeks and months of ministry by hundreds (maybe thousands) of people. So it is with almost any ministry, whether it be backyard Bible clubs or food for the hungry programs.

3. *The daily stress and strain of ministry requires the moral, physical, and spiritual support of a partner.* Doing a ministry alone could burn you out.

A classic example is the prophet Elijah. There is no more dramatic account of a powerful man of God than the scene of Elijah on Mt. Carmel facing the hundreds of prophets of Baal (1 Kings 18). Yet very shortly afterward he cowered before Jezebel's vengeance and fled into a cave to hide. At that point Elijah surely could have used a ministry partner for encouragement, support, and a sharing of responsibility. The Lord confronted Elijah and thrust him out of his protective cave. He reminded Elijah that he was not the only faithful one in the land. There were seven thousand others.

Notice how often Paul acknowledged his ministry partners:

- The letter of 1 Corinthians was sent by Paul and "Sosthenes our brother."
- In 1 Corinthians 16:17-18, Paul acknowledges that Stephanas, Fortunatus, and Achaicus have "refreshed his spirit."
- Second Corinthians was sent by Paul and Timothy, "our brother."
- Philippians 2:25 mentions that Epaphroditus ministered to Paul's needs.
- In Colossians 4:10-11 we learn that Aristarchus, Mark, and Justus "proved to be an encouragement" to Paul.
- First Thessalonians came from Paul, Silvanus, and Timothy.

- A glance at 2 Timothy 4:9-12 shows those partners who deserted Paul, who stood by him, and those (Timothy and Mark) whom Paul wanted with him.
- Romans 16 shows Paul's dependence on others and his gratitude for their ministry.

Ministry in this world is, in reality, a spiritual battle. It is often tough, grueling, and tiring. The risk is too great to attempt it alone.

4. *We need ministry partners to provide us with a proper perspective of our effectiveness and accomplishments.* Failure, as well as success, is difficult for humans to handle well.

Jerry is a businessman in our town. He is also a Christian with a burden for other businessmen. He decided to begin an early morning Bible study at one of the local coffee shops. He spent weeks arranging all the details. A place was secured, special features and speakers were arranged, letters of personal invitation were sent out. On the given day Jerry arrived at the coffee shop to discover he was the only one there.

Exactly why the program failed is not the issue. The fact is that Jerry, working alone, sharing the planning and design with no one, was forced to bear all the brunt of failure. He withdrew from any ministry for several months. Not only could he have used someone to stand alongside him for encouragement, but an additional ministry may have added additional gifts needed to make the project successful.

The opposite is just as true. Outstanding success in a personal ministry has destroyed more than one person's effectiveness. If you are playing a solo game and win, you will tend to accept all the honor and glory. That might be all right in the sports or entertainment fields, but not in Christian ministry. The Lord is to receive all glory and praise for any success we might have.

Self-acclaim is a very easy and sometimes subtle trap when you minister alone. After all, you think, you did all the planning, all the work; then you should get the rewards. You assume it was your own power that accomplished the task.

Psalm 106:32-33 reminds us that this attitude caused Moses to sin at Meribah. In his anger at the lack of trust the people had in the Lord, he spoke rashly, as though the power to bring forth water from the rock were his own and the people were rebelling against him, rather than God. He confused the Lord's power with his own. Such a mistake caused him to fail to enter the promised land.

5. *We have a better chance of finding God's will and plan for our ministry with the prayer support of others.* We can confirm God's will for our lives by several means. The Lord speaks directly to our hearts. We are convinced He wants us to accomplish a certain act. That can then be confirmed by the Holy Spirit's speaking through the Scriptures. That is, what we have decided to do makes scriptural sense. Finally, we can receive confirmation from our Christian brothers and sisters, as they, too, seek God's will for us.

Notice in Acts 6:1-6 that the apostles' decision to add to the leadership of the Jerusalem church was confirmed by the whole congregation. When the Lord first called out Paul and Barnabas to be those first missionaries, that call was confirmed by Simeon, Lucius, and Manaen (Acts 13:1-3). Paul's Macedonian vision to take the gospel to Europe was confirmed immediately by his traveling companions (Acts 16:7-10).

Ministry partners can help you discover and keep in tune with God's will.

Ministry partners come in various sizes and shapes and by different means. I happened to marry mine. Neither of us were Christians at the time and, of course, had no idea that we would ever know God, let alone desire to serve Him. But it was His will to call my wife and me together, first to Himself, then into His ministry. We marched hand in hand through the university and seminary years and then into the pastorate. I find I need other ministry partners too.

How do you go about finding ministry partners?

1. Define the ministry situation as you see it. What exactly would this partner of yours be doing? Write it out clearly.

Communication is impossible if we cannot even articulate the job description.

Here is an example:

My ministry partner will be responsible for assisting me to teach the second grade class at our Sunday school. He will need to spend about 6 hours a week at this task, 3 hours per week in study and preparation of curriculum, 1½ hours each Saturday with me in lesson review and room preparation, 1½ hours in class time. In addition, we will spend one Saturday afternoon per month visiting in the students' homes. Once each quarter my partner will assist me with the planning and implementation of a class party. During my absence because of sickness or vacation, my partner will be in charge of the class. The purpose of this ministry is to expose these second graders to persons who are actively living out the Christian life and to teach them accounts and principles in the Bible that will lead them to Christ and help them grow in Him.

2. List all the gifts, talents, and ministries that are needed to perform the job.

In the case above, you might list:

    a) the gift of teaching
    b) patience
    c) creative artistic ability
    d) basic background of Bible knowledge
    e) dependability
    f) punctuality
    g) warmth and sincerity
    h) sensitivity to needs of children
    i) musical talent
    j) proved ability to complete assigned tasks
    k) other

Once you have an exhaustive list, you will want to place in order those qualifications. Which ones are absolute necessities? Which are somewhat important? Which less important? When you have carefully done that, then and only then are you ready to think about who that partner will be.

3. Bring your lists to the Lord in prayer and ask Him to show you who might qualify.

Make a list of possibilities, people you know that most closely exhibit these qualities, regardless of their present involvements. Consider only those who would be the best for the job. If absolutely no one comes to mind, then hold on to your statement of qualities. Do not compromise. Wait for the Lord to bring someone new into your life or to prompt memory of someone you have overlooked. If you do have a list, place your number one choice first.

Take this list to God. Ask Him to show you any reason your number one choice should not be asked. Determine that, no matter what, you will not accept just anyone. Be selective. Do not be in a hurry.

4. Once you are convinced you have made a good choice, personally ask the person to assist you. Carefully present him with the job description, its purpose, the qualities you believe are needed, and why you feel he is the right choice. Encourage him to ask questions, but do not force him to make an instant decision. Give him time to pray and consider the possibilities. That is your best assurance that the Lord will confirm His will.

If the person eventually declines, go to another one on your list. If you have no one else to ask, perhaps the Lord expects you to continue this ministry alone, or He will provide assistance at a future time, or, if it is impossible to do this particular ministry alone, perhaps He is telling you that this ministry should not be done at all at this time.

Success in ministry is available to all of God's children. The Lord wants you to prosper in the tasks that He assigns to you. And there is the very good chance that He wants you to share that prosperity and success with someone else.

8

Try the Door Just One More Time

Christians have for years talked about the "second touch" of the blind man of Bethsaida. But, little has been said of the "second knock" of the Syrophoenician woman (Mark 7:24-30).

Jesus had just completed a tiring ministry to the multitudes. He hoped to give both Himself and the disciples a time of rest and recuperation, away from the interruption of faithful followers and curiosity seekers.

They crossed the boundary into the neighboring district of Tyre. Here they hoped for the anonymity of a home or inn. Yet, the notoriety of the miracle worker from Nazareth could not be contained within the provincial Roman borders. While he reclined in the home of a gracious host, a woman, known only by her nationality, came looking for the prophet.

She was troubled, humble, and persistent. She had reason to be troubled: her daughter suffered from demonic possession. So, laying aside the customs of the culture of her day, she entered this home and broke up its quiet atmosphere.

As she faced Jesus, she fell to the floor in worship. This woman was not Jewish, nor was she a proselyte, nor was she called a "God-fearer." If she had bowed in worship before, it was probably to a chunk of molded metal or finely polished wood. Now she begged, prostrate before this man, on behalf of her daughter.

If she was persistent in her request, Jesus was just as persistent in declining. He kept saying, "Let the children be satisfied first, for it is not good to take the children's bread and throw it to the dogs."

When we hear that response coming from Jesus, we often cringe. We would like to think He never said such a thing. Do those words really advocate ethnic slurs and bigotry? Hardly! But, they do tell us something about persistent faith and our reasonable God.

Before we become too offended by the language Jesus used, we must understand what the people were actually hearing. First, we are dealing at this point with the very heart of election. God chose the Jews to receive the ministry of Jesus. From the time of Cain and Abel until this present day, election, or God's singling out a particular person or people, is a central theme of His revelation to us.

Second, Jesus said, "Let the children be satisfied first." This is not to mean that it would never be proper to reach out and incorporate the non-Jew. It meant, rather, that it was not the time for such an event to take place. In Matthew 10:5, Jesus instructed the twelve not to enter any Samaritan city. But in Acts 1:8 the resurrected Christ said plainly that Samaria is a part of the world-wide mission field. It is therefore, a matter of timing and planning.

Third, the term Jesus used has to do with a puppy or household pet, rather than with the wild dogs of the streets that Jews most often associated with Gentiles.

There must have been some encouragement in the inflection of His voice, for the woman did not hesitate to respond to His rebuff. Was it the desperate condition of her daughter, her own shrewdness, or the look of hope in His eyes that caused her to inquire further? Whichever the case, her diligence paid off. Her daughter was healed. In fact, said Jesus, it was because of her answer that He relented.

It was a costly change of mind for Jesus. He knew how quickly the news would spread through the land. He knew crowds from far and wide would line up for a miracle touch. Their seclusion was ended; they must return to Galilee. But the lessons the disciples learned from that experience may have been more important than seclusion.

We often symbolically speak of God's "opening the doors"

of service, blessing, provision. Some say that Matthew 7:8, ". . . To him who knocks it shall be opened," means that we should attempt to travel down certain corridors of life letting God open doors. A closed door signifies, we say, that God's will is to be found elsewhere. Yet, the closed door did not hinder the Syrophoenician woman from knocking one more time, and that time it opened.

Jesus did not reward her for her perseverance as much as He did for her wisdom. He liked her answer. If we feel compelled, as that woman did, to persist in the face of the customary etiquette of taking no for an answer, we must come before God with reasons.

We serve a reasonable God. He asks that we use our full reasoning ability as we approach Him with a request. Like a loving Father to an eager child He asks, "Why?"

The Syrophoenician woman is not alone in not taking no for an answer. Moses repeated his request to behold God's glory (Exodus 33). Abraham actually seemed to barter with God as he interceded for Sodom (Genesis 18). Hezekiah was told that he would die but sought God for another answer and was granted fifteen more years (2 Kings 20). Even Mary, mother of Jesus, refused to let alone the issue concerning the lack of wine at the wedding feast at Cana. When Jesus replied, "Woman, what do I have to do with you? My hour has not yet come" (John 2), Mary replied by sending the servants over to do whatever He told them. She knocked a second time.

Several years ago as an enthusiastic and idealistic young seminarian, I had an opportunity to serve as temporary pulpit supply in a church that was searching for a pastor. Impetuous as I was, I stopped one night in front of that dark and empty sanctuary and literally knocked on the huge wooden double doors.

"Lord," I cried, as I rapped repeatedly, "You said if we knock, You will open. So, I'm knocking. I ask that You open this church up so that I can be called to serve as the regular pastor when I graduate in June."

At the time it seemed like a reasonable request. As the pastor-

seeking committee began thinking along the same lines, I felt
sure the door was opening. But, *slam!* The door quickly shut
tight. Denominational rules stated that an interim, or temporary, supply was not eligible to be called as permanent pastor
of the church he was serving. Besides, I was told, the church
definitely had its problems, and they needed a more experienced
man at the helm.

So I asked the Lord again. No banging on the sanctuary
door this time. Rather, I stated my reasons: "Lord, I'm a
country boy with a country boy's manners and speech. This is
a country town. They trust me. Lord, they need aggressive,
creative leadership, not merely a sustaining one. Let me come
and try my million and one seminary-induced ideas. Father,
my heart is burdened for the people in this town. Let me try
to reach some."

As I would think of a new reason I quickly took it to Him.
Then, just as unexpectedly as their closing, the doors began to
open. An escape clause about seminary students doing approved field work began the process.

A few days after graduation I was ordained and installed as
the pastor, and fruitful, happy years of ministry followed.

The question that comes to mind whenever we consider that
at times we might ask God a second time is, "Why?" Why
would God need to be asked again? We certainly believe that
God knows the desires of our hearts before we ask Him. We
also know that He is ready to answer us even more willingly
than a loving, earthly father. Why is it that sometimes (not
always, of course) He makes us repeat the requests all over
again?

There are several possibilities. For one thing, momentary
rejection forces us to examine closely the desires of our own
hearts. The parent who rushes out to buy the very first Christmas present his child mentions in August is acting foolishly.
Every wise Mom and Dad know that you wait until the child
is consistent about wanting one certain gift. It is not that the
parent is unloving; it is merely that he wants to wait and determine what the child "really" wants. Waiting means the child

will get the sincere desire of his or her heart. (Even with the waiting, parents often find the "got-to-have-it" present abandoned by February.)

In our enthusiasm to serve the Lord, we might ask Him something rather impulsively. His initial refusal is a way to say, "Are you sure you really want that?" By forcing us to reexamine our request, He helps us purify our motives and strengthen our reasoning processes.

In addition, I believe that God waits until the second petition in order to increase our total trust in His ability to provide for us. At times we have our life plans all schemed out and only present them to the Lord for His official, perfunctory blessing. In such a case the Lord is telling us, "Wait a minute. If this thing works at all, it will be because of My doing. Remember?" Often it is only after our big ideas for success and greatness fail that we cast ourselves on the Lord and rely totally on His provision and strength.

How do you go about asking God for something after He has already told you no?

1. *Examine your own motives.* Why do you want Him to grant your request? Is it strictly for your own benefit? Can you truthfully say it would advance His Kingdom, honor His name, bring Him glory? Is it something at the heart of your life's ministry, or is it just a little added trivia that "would be nice"?

2. *Prayerfully present every reason for the necessity of this request's being granted.* Actually write down the reasons. Show them to a mature Christian friend. See if they make sense to him. If you cannot convince a friend or are too ashamed of your reasons to show them, perhaps you had better forget the whole thing. Remember, our Lord is a reasonable God. And do not be afraid to tell Him all the deep longings of your heart.

3. *Ask clearly for direct, measurable answers.* The Syrophoenician woman knew exactly what she wanted: her daughter delivered. Moses knew what he wanted: to behold God's glory. Hezekiah knew what he wanted: more years of life. Mary knew

what she wanted: more wine for the wedding celebration. I knew exactly what I wanted: to be pastor of a particular church. How will you know when God answers your request? Look for and expect Him to provide in a clearly defined way.

4. *Wait before God until you receive an answer.* Do not "hang up the phone" before He has a chance to reply.

God speaks in differing ways. We can never confine Him to any one method or process. Yet it is reasonable for us to expect an answer. He is not insensitive nor disinterested. He was quite willing to enter into dialogue with the lady from Syrophoenicia. Likewise, He is willing to hold spiritual conversations with us.

There is no guarantee, however, that His final answer will be any different from the first one. Paul asked three times to have that thorn of Satan removed. Three times the Lord said no. It would be a mistake to think that we never get a yes on the first try too. We have all tasted the joy of that experience.

Every once in a while He might be testing our real desires and our faith by insisting that we ask a second time. We should not think that such a request is offending Him. We need not hesitate to knock again at the door that seems closed. But when we come the second time, let us lay aside the emotionalism of the immediate moment and come supplied with a clear, reasoned support for why our heavenly Father should fulfill our requests.

That "second knock" might be the only thing standing between you and the success you are looking for.

9

Shortcut to Success[*]

The road to success can often be a long, tiring road. How would you like to know a shortcut? Sound good? It is good, but definitely not easy.

In Mark 8 we hit the pinnacle of Jesus' revelation to His disciples. Peter spoke out the truth of eternity when he said, "Thou are the Christ." Now that they understood this, they were ready for hard-core discipleship teaching.

Immediately Jesus began to tell them exactly how He would "suffer many things and be rejected by the elders and the chief priests and the scribes, and be killed, and after three days rise again." The disciples, once again led by Peter, were quite indignant with such talk. Surely no such thing would happen!

At that point it is as if Jesus drew a line across that dusty Palestine roadway and said, "This is what it will take to be My disciple. Don't bother crossing the line unless you're willing to go all out." What He said in actuality was, "If anyone wishes to come after Me, let him deny himself, and take up his cross and follow Me. For whoever wishes to save his life shall lose it; and whoever loses his life for My sake and the gospel's shall save it" (vv. 34-35).

That challenge is at the very heart of any dream or desire you ever had for achieving spiritual success and greatness in this life. It separates the potential from the actual, the thinkers from the doers, the spectators from the players. Jesus is calling to radical Christian discipleship.

*Originally titled "How To Be a Radical Without Joining a Cult." Reprinted from HIS, student magazine of the Inter-Varsity Christian Fellowship, U.S.A.

What does that mean for us? First, let us define some terms:

- *Disciple*—one who receives instruction from another; a follower of one particular person
- *Discipline*—self-controlled instruction; training of the mind, body, and spirit in subjection to an authority
- *Christian discipleship*—subjecting one's life-style to the systematic training of mind, body, and spirit in order to conform to the life and teachings of Jesus Christ
- *Radical Christian discipleship*—progressing from talking about it to doing it

Every so often in the history of Christianity there comes a period of time that produces an outcrop of radical Christian disciples—Saint Francis and his followers with their vows of chastity and poverty; Luther, Calvin, Zwingli, and other Reformers; the Wesleys, Whitefield, and the Oxford Club; and the Student Missionary Movement of the turn of the century are all examples. What separated those believers from others in their day was their undying effort to be "doers of the Word." Today we would call them fanatics, overreligious zealots, radicals. Yet the call of Christ has always been a radical call.

Luke 14:26-27 certainly does not tell us everything we need to know about discipleship, but note the radical nature of Christ's words: "If anyone comes to Me, and does not hate his own father and mother and wife and children and brothers and sisters, yes, and even his own life, he cannot be My disciple. Whoever does not carry his own cross and come after Me cannot be My disciple."

Here is no wishy-washy, half-hearted plea for volunteers. It is an all-or-nothing challenge for qualification. Far too many of us come as the rich young ruler, wanting all the benefits but unwilling to make the sacrifices. The question in my mind is, Why are there so few radical disciples?

The roll call of radical disciples is not limited to the "Holy Hundred" who have an extra dispensation of devotion. This is not a plateau for the elite, but the common footing expected of all Christ's followers. Perhaps it does not happen because we seek to build the Lord's army on the lowest common denominator, which produces a ragtag, undisciplined, unaccountable lot that is less effective against the kingdom of Satan than Don Quixote against the windmills. The free gift of salvation does not bring with it the automatic prize of a disciplined life. Yet is that not what our hearts cry out for?

"I know I am not the Christian I should be . . ." "I know I shouldn't be this way . . ." "Actually, I'd really like to serve the Lord better, but . . ."

Most of us desire to be about our Father's work in a meaningful way. We find ourselves saying, "I must give more to God—more time, more talent, more effort."

As the Body of Christ we have too often failed to challenge those with such longings. We have set our goals and standards so low that we have been cursed by getting exactly what we aimed for.

Years ago Douglas Hyde brought out this fault clearly in his book *Dedication and Leadership* (South Bend, Ind.: Notre Dame, 1964), page 27.

> The communists make far bigger demands upon their people than the average Christian organization would ever dare to make. As I have already noted, they believe that if you make big demands upon people you will get a big response. So this is made a deliberate policy on their part. They never make the small demand if they can make the big one.

The Communists are not the only group to demand and secure voluntary sacrificial service for their cause. In recent years hordes of cultic groups have systematically sniped at the ranks of Christianity. Many young people with high levels of leadership potential follow the beat of a different and dangerous drummer. It is surely not the irrational and nonsensical theology that attracts so many. Is it not rather the single-minded devotion and discipline required of all who are dedicated to the cause that is so attractive?

I believe it is possible and desirable to be a radical disciple of Jesus Christ without necessarily leaving your family, your school, your job, or historic evangelical Christianity. The suggestions that follow are bare minimum beginnings. Your particular call will involve other areas as well. This is not an easy course. It is strictly for the serious, the deep water swimmers.

If you are one of those Sunday morning hodads, basking in the sun of spiritual security, if you have never gone farther than holding to the raft and kicking your feet, or if you are one of those surf chasers who run back and forth with each new wave, perhaps now is the time to see if you really have what it takes. Push yourself beyond the sound of the breakers and begin to experience the excitement of a life of swimming in deep waters.

Consider the following steps to radical discipleship:

1. *Develop a radical prayer life.*

How do I get started? (1) Grab your television schedule and circle your favorite program each night. When the hour comes, turn off the television, get to a quiet place, and pray. (2) Buy a yearly appointment calendar to use strictly as a prayer request book. Write down each day what you pray for, then write the answers as they come. (3) Each week share an answered prayer with three Christian friends and one non-Christian friend.

What will it cost? (1) Your favorite television programs. (2) The knees of your pants. (3) Several of your friends and relatives will harass you for "going overboard." (4) About $3.50 for a yearly appointment calendar.

What will I get out of it? (1) Peace, knowing that God is in charge. (2) Heartaches, tears for the needs of this world. (3) Excitement, finding out God really does answer your prayers.

2. *Develop a habit of radical Bible study.*

How do I get started? (1) Set your alarm to *loud* and place three feet beyond arm's reach from the bed. Set time for one hour earlier than usual. (2) Sit down with proper reference tools and *study* (not merely read) two Old Testament chapters and two New Testament chapters every day of the year. (3) Look for and share with someone a new spiritual insight per day.

What will it cost? (1) One hour of sleep per day. (2) The price of a leather study Bible, Bible dictionary, Bible handbook, concordance, and notebook. (3) Your morning newspaper.

What will I get out of it? (1) Confusion, for you will find answers you do not even know the questions for yet. (2) Instructions on how to live a radical day. (3) Insight, for you will begin to understand why things happen the way they do.

3. *Join a radical fellowship.*

What does it look like? (1) Prayerfully seek out, discover, and join with others who are interested in radical discipleship. (2) Meet for potluck dinner once a week. (3) Share discoveries, mistakes, needs, and join together in service.

How much will it cost? (1) About three hours per week. (2) All your pride and egotism. (3) Your ideas of independence and self-sufficiency.

What will I get? (1) Family—a dozen friends who become closer than relatives. (2) Support—others who will sink or swim to stay by your side. (3) Expanded ministry—achieving goals no one individual could accomplish.

4. *Develop a radical witness.*

What does it look like? (1) Make a list of all people you come in contact with daily (everyone!). Make a check next to repeat contacts. (2) Tally up the week's total. Highest number of checks indicate your prime targets for witness. (3) Relate to these persons your own testimony and the seed of the gospel (the life, death, and resurrection of Jesus). (4) Ask them to respond.

How much will it cost? (1) One of your closest friends will quit sending you Christmas cards. (2) Tony down the street will not let your dog play with his dog. (3) At least twice a week you will notice someone crossing the street to avoid seeing you.

What will I get? (1) Rejection, for the children of darkness do not like light. (2) Joy, as you see lives changed. (3) New friends, in gratitude for your boldness in sharing Jesus with them.

5. *Start a sacrificial ministry.*

What does it look like? (1) Every payday write a check for 10 percent of your income and send to your church, fellowship, mission. (2) Fast three meals per week (your choice) and send money saved to a hunger relief organization. (3) Write, phone, or make a visit of support and encouragement to one missionary, preacher, Christian leader, or friend per week.

How much will it cost? (1) Minimum of 10 percent of every penny you make. (2) Three meals per week. (3) One half hour per week, plus stamps and stationery.

What will I get? (1) Freedom, in learning how to possess money, instead of its possessing you. (2) Purpose, in knowing you are a part of something bigger, something meaningful and important. (3) An expanded world view of God's giving power.

10

Life with That Extra Zest

I once received a birthday card that stated,"You are the dill pickle on the hamburger of life." That is not exactly scriptural, but it does remind us that Jesus expects us to be society's salt. "Salt is good; but if the salt becomes unsalty, with what will you make it salty again? Have salt in yourselves, and be at peace with one another" (Mark 9:50). Even a casual reading of the Sermon on the Mount in Matthew 5, 6, and 7 shows that Jesus clearly saw His followers as the "salt of the earth." In our desire to achieve spiritual greatness, we must understand and enact this principle of "saltiness." What does a salty life look like?

One of the most common uses for salt at the dinner table is to bring out the full flavor of everything it touches. A solid, committed Christian life in the midst of society should bring out the taste—that is, bring out the best and most positive qualities of that society and its people.

Before Margaret began to teach health at Lakewood High School, she was warned that there were open hostilities among the teaching staff. Over the past several years of rather fierce salary negotiations, two rival groups appeared. One group, the "traditionalists," seemed always to support the superintendent. They seldom felt like pushing hard for increased benefits. The others, the "activists," were vocally insistent that conditions and programs and salary schedules be radically updated.

The tensions were most sharply felt by the teachers during the morning break and lunch period when they gathered in the teachers' lounge. The two groups constantly made cutting re-

marks back and forth. After only a few days in that environ-
ment, Margaret was ready to volunteer for permanent yard
duty. But she did not. Instead, she chose to be the salt.

During the day she purposely searched for positive, construc-
tive, creatives things that were going on at Lakewood. With at
least one of those things in mind she would enter the lounge
and immediately steer the conversation toward that positive
factor about the school, its teachers, its programs, and even its
administration. Sometimes Margaret would talk to one group,
sometimes the other.

Because she was new on the staff, many times what she
thought was new and innovative was actually an old, well
established program that everyone at Lakewood took for
granted. When she excitedly told her co-workers what a wonderful thing Mr. Miller was doing with the band—how he vis-
ited every one of the band members and carefully spelled out
the plans, goals, and visions for the band with each parent—
they quickly assured her that Mr. Miller had been doing that
for years. Yet, as they thought about it, they were reminded
of its uniqueness and effectiveness. Miller *did* do a fine job
with the Lakewood Lancer Band. They spent nearly ten minutes discussing the band's highlights over the past years, for a
time forgetting that Mr. Miller was one of those "others."

It was not an easy task being salt under those circumstances.
However, Margaret persevered. At first, many of her colleagues
either chuckled or sneered at her idealism and enthusiasm.
Now, three years later, everyone notices the difference. The
teachers' break time is more a friendly, uplifting visiting session. To be sure, there are still divisions over contract nego-
tations, but life is definitely more pleasant and relaxed around
Lakewood High since Margaret began adding the salt.

In the days when the New Testament was written, salt was
the most common form of preservative available. Meat could
last long periods of time if properly preserved in salt. For Jesus
to ask His followers to have salt in themselves must have also
meant they were to prevent spiritual and moral decay around

them. There is right in the world; there is wrong. It is based on God's revealed Word. The followers of Jesus must see that right is preserved and wrong is held in check.

The Roman world, at the time of the early Christians, did not have a very high value of human life. The father of the family had supreme say over life and death. A newborn baby that displeased him in some way could be discarded upon the village garbage pile with no legal or social restrictions.

Christian morality deplored such a thing. If God formed us in our mother's wombs, if He designed our lives before the world began, if He planted His divine image in each one, then every little life is vitally important. A cheap view of life is immoral and must be countered. So, the Christians scoured the dumps and trash heaps, rescuing the babies and raising them as their own. The Christian influence eliminated that practice eventually. (Now, I wonder, is it rearing its ugly head again under the nice banner of "human rights" and "free choice"?)

We are still called upon to be the salt of our society. We need to make an open, honest stand for what is right. We need to slow down the gradual decay of our society, country, and world. There is no freedom from responsibility just because we foresee end times and know everything will be corrupt anyway. Many devout Christians believe they will be taken up out of this apostate world and never face the horrible hardships of the Tribulation, but even a rapture is no excuse for us to refrain from an all-out effort to stem the tide of evil and promote the cause of good.

There is a time for everyone to stand up and say: "Abortion is wrong!" "Corrupt government is wrong!" "Discrimination is wrong!" "Homosexuality is wrong!" "Mass destruction of races is wrong!"

"But," you say, "why get involved? We are so few. What difference could we really make anyway?"

All the difference in the world. It does not take much salt to preserve a lot of meat. Just a little active salt can work its way into every cell of that roast. A few salty Christians could affect an entire community. It would have taken only ten faithful to change the outcome of the infamous city of Sodom (Genesis 18).

How many will it take in your town? Are you willing to be one of them? This is a tough hurdle that many of us would like to ignore. Ignore it we would, too, if it were not for the fact that this challenge stands right in the middle of our pathway to true spiritual success.

A third way we can be salt is by adding zest and excitement to an otherwise dull world. Salt is a spice. It not only brings out the natural flavor of whatever it touches, but it also adds its own distinct taste. That is why we ask for salt, not nutmeg, for our hot, buttered corn on the cob.

That concept may seem strange because most often the non-Christian thinks of the Christian life-style as dull, flat, boring. The Christians are those who are always putting a damper on anyone trying to have a good time. It is not surprising that they think that. What is surprising is that so many Christians believe it themselves.

Somehow we have surrendered our ability to make life adventuresome and have left the world to struggle on its own to find purpose, meaning, joy. We cram our lives with human gimmicks, fads, cults, and crazes in a futile attempt to "enjoy life." If all that still does not satisfy, we cover up the disappointment with alcohol, television, or drugs.

The most exciting place to be on the face of the earth some two thousand years ago was not the Colosseum in Rome. It was not at the sporting events in Athens or on a boat trip down the Nile. Without question, the real adventure was taking place on the rocky Palestinian hillsides. Jesus' close companions were never bored. They lived active, fulfilling lives, following Him as He carried out His ministry. The whole book of Mark is a vivid account of adventure. There was no yawning when He walked across the water. There were no blank stares of disinterest when He called Lazarus from the tomb. There were no spring daydreams while He delivered the "but

I say unto you" sayings during the Sermon on the Mount. Things happened when you traveled with Jesus.

The early church found that to be true for even the second and third generations of Christians. Luke's narrative of Acts could as easily be called "The Adventures of Early Christians." But what label could be put on your present life? Perhaps "The Daily Rut of an Average Christian"?

The disciples had three things in their favor:

1. *They went wherever Jesus went.* They followed Him; He did not follow them. If He dined at the house of a tax collector, they did too. If He attended a wedding celebration, so did they. They stood alongside Him in all His anger as He cleared the Temple. They were there to see His tender compassion when He lifted Jairus's daughter back to life. Certainly there were times when they found themselves in places they would never have chosen for themselves. They followed after Jesus.

Today it is the same. We cannot control Him. We cannot keep Him in our beautiful church buildings. He keeps popping out into the streets of skid row or into unfamiliar homes. He leads us to the strangest people, into the most complicated relationships, usually with the most surprising results. Do not be satisfied with an occasional "visit" from the Lord. Get out of your spiritual easy chair and follow Him, wherever He goes.

2. *They learned to let Him do whatever He wanted to do.* C. S. Lewis keeps reminding us in the Narnia tales that Aslan is not a tame lion. He cannot be controlled nor his actions totally predicted by humans. We must allow Jesus the freedom to do what He wants. He will, of course, do it anyway. But, if we fail to accept what He is doing, just because it does not fit into some preconceived idea, we will miss much of the excitement of discipleship. Some are only content with a tame, controllable Jesus. How boring.

3. *They learned that instant obedience to Christ's commands brought dramatic results.* It is not always easy to obey. There must have been some feelings of foolishness as they began to pass out five small loaves of bread to five thousand people. What an event that turned out to be!

Remember the disciples' going into town to find an animal for Jesus to ride as He entered Jerusalem? He told them, "Go into the village opposite you, and immediately as you enter it, you will find a colt tied there, on which no one yet has ever sat; untie it and bring it here. And if anyone says to you, 'Why are you doing this?' you say, 'The Lord has need of it,' and immediately he will send it back here" (Mark 11:2-3).

It sounds almost like stealing. They, of course, do not fully understand all that Jesus knows. Verse 6 points out that they were confronted by people who questioned why they were leading off this colt, and they replied "just as Jesus had told them."

They may have thought it, but we do not see them searching for a "rent-a-colt" service, nor do we see them going door-to-door asking for a donkey. They did not even search for the owner of the colt. They merely did everything exactly as they were told. What an unforgettable day that was.

Christians are the salt, the spice, the taste of life. It takes work to cover up that taste and make life boring. Jesus warned His disciples that there was a danger of losing their saltiness (Mark 9:50). It is a very current warning. Every disciple in every age must continue striving for that Christian distinctive that makes him different from the rest of the world. To lose that is to be as worthless as "saltless" salt.

One way we can lose our saltiness is through solidification. A solid block of salt might be all right for cattle to lick, but it is of no value in a salt shaker. The Lord wants our saltiness sprinkled throughout the community. It is possible for Christians to have such a narrow view of life that they literally never get beyond the four walls of the church. Day after day, week after week, year after year, they come in contact with only other Christians. They work with Christians, visit with Christians, socialize with Christians, and (it is hoped) live with Christians. If there is no exposure to anything but Christians, the salt begins to solidify. People trap themselves in a Christian ghetto.

An opposite problem is overexposure. We are in constant battle against the world, the flesh, and the devil. We fight back with our saltiness. Yet if we fail to replenish our supply, all our work can be neutralized. Christian fellowship, study, and worship are needed to restore our saltiness, but only in the tasteless, purposeless, drab world can we really use up our salt.

How can you make sure you are acting as salt?

1. List the three areas of greatest moral, physical, or spiritual concern in your community (or school, or neighborhood, or work, etc.)

    a)

    b)

    c)

2. What do you believe is the correct scriptural response to those situations?

3. I will personally respond to those conditions by

    a) writing, telling, and/or phoning the following influential people about my views on this matter.

       (1)   (2)   (3)

    b) praying every _____ for _____ minutes about it.

    c) promising to continue to be the salt in this situation until the following result takes place:

_____

_____

_____

11

Your Limitless Possibilities

Everyone who ever remotely considered a total commitment to Jesus Christ has spent some time trying to decide, "Just exactly what kind of work does He want me to do?" And I am sure mentally, if not physically, you have made a list of the possibilities. Likewise, most people consider the impossibilities as well. There are some things (many things!) you are sure you would never be able to do.

Maybe your lists would look something like this:

Possible Ministries	*Impossible Ministries*
Visit new residents	Minister to bereaved
Teach adult class	Teach junior high class
Lead couples group	Lead cross-cultural evangelism
Be church janitor	Preach a sermon
Be volunteer hospital worker	Work in Ugandan hospital
Sing in the choir	Direct vacation Bible school
Pray for missionaries	Pray in front of whole church
Host home Bible Study	Be houseparent for ex-addicts
Serve hot meals to senior citizens	Do door-to-door evangelism
Prepare church bulletin board	Build a church in New Guinea

Whatever your particular lists include, most of us have already determined what things are within our capabilities and which are not. However, the spiritual ministry that is to have a lasting impact on your world will more often come from the right hand column rather than the left hand column.

The possibilities list is usually the area where most people spend their time and efforts. And they can often succeed. The trouble is, they usually succeed on their own strength. True spiritual success and greatness can never come about solely on human strength. Your taste of true greatness, success with a purpose, will come only as you overcome your fears and jump headlong into a project or ministry where you must wholly, completely, and desperately trust in God's provision. Most of us lack the spiritual boldness to try such a venture. We settle for Christian mediocrity or living on the "safe side."

Jesus' disciples first began learning that principle when the rich young ruler came to visit. He had just left the apostolic band, dejected because he was unwilling to give up his wealth to follow Jesus. With a sense of pity Jesus said, "How hard it will be for those who are wealthy to enter the kingdom of God!" (Mark 10:23).

That is not such a startling statement to our ears these days. We are familiar with warnings of the corruption of riches. However, look again at the scene.

Here was a man who honestly and sincerely had tried his best to keep every commandment. That included not only the scriptural commands but also the teaching of the scribes. If he failed, I am sure he went through the proper atonement procedure of the sacrificial system. He came to Jesus seeking God. In addition, in the minds of the disciples, the very fact that such an outwardly holy man was wealthy, too, proved that he was right with God. After all, was it not the righteous that was blessed by God with material goods? Now, saturated with this cultural thinking, we see how strange Jesus' words seemed to them.

In verses 24 and 25, Jesus reiterated to the astonished disciples how difficult it is for the rich to enter the Kingdom of God. At this point His followers threw up their hands in bewilderment and exclaimed, "Then who can be saved?" (Mark 10:26).

In their minds Jesus had closed the door of salvation to every man. If a person who did all the right things, lived a good life, and exhibited the obvious blessings of God could not make it to heaven, then, no matter what they did, they could not make it either. Jesus responded, in effect, "You're right. No one is going to make it—on his own strength. But it is not impossible with God's strength, for all things are possible with God."

The point is there is nothing a man can do to achieve salvation. He could have everything in the world in his favor, yet not succeed. But if God decides to work in his life, there is no way to keep him out of heaven.

This is a principle of ministry as well as salvation. Our Lord is in the business of doing the humanly impossible. He is looking for people who will trust Him to work in impossible ways. If the Kingdom of God only progressed at the rate of human achievement, then it would take billions of epochs to accomplish His work. On the other hand, if He could find a few men and women who would yield themselves to His divine power, then a tremendous amount could be accomplished in only a short time.

There are two key factors to remember as you begin to think out the direction of your possible (or impossible) ministry. First, the self-made man concept is not at all scriptural. It is an appealing, idealistic, American fantasy that people can make themselves into whatever they want. It seldom happens in the material world, and it never happens in the spiritual world. The idea of self-promoted success goes against the very heart and core of true discipleship.

Listen again to Jesus' words:

> For whoever wishes to save his life shall lose it; and whoever loses his life for My sake and the gospel's shall save it. [Mark 8:35]

> Whoever wishes to become great among you shall be your servant. [Mark 10:43]

> For everyone who exalts himself shall be humbled, and he who humbles himself shall be exalted. [Luke 14:11]

I do not believe Jesus said those words to humiliate us. He

was not trying to crush us. Quite the opposite. He knows all
about our desires for success. He knows that we want to make
an impact on our world. He would just like to show us the way.
We will not have any idea of the thrill and satisfaction of true
spiritual ministry until we have moved beyond trust in our own
strength. Greatness—that is, success with a purpose—comes
only through the power of God. Any other success will be a
shallow and unfulfilling substitute.

It might seem that God does not want us to do anything at
all—that we just sit back and some magical power works
through us, in spite of us. That is not true. The second thing
you must remember is this: our job is to be in the right place,
at the right time, and in the right attitude.

1. *The right place.* God is everywhere. Yet He is not doing
everything everywhere. Most pastors and church leaders know
that all too well. As soon as word spreads across the country
of an exciting new evangelism program that is proving successful, thousands of churches immediately copy the program. Some
succeed, many others carefully go through all the right motions
and utterly fail. Why? Often it is because it just is not the
Lord's program for that particular place.

The Gobi desert might not be the place to build a glass
cathedral, and Anaheim, California, just might not be the best
location to translate the New Testament into Mongolian. All
the faith and dependence in the Lord you can muster will not
help if you are in the wrong place.

In the late sixties and early seventies a successful method of
reaching young people was the coffee house ministry. I know;
I ran one. We were located in northeast Los Angeles. There, on
that busy city boulevard, street kids would wander down the
stairs to our place and listen to a new phenomenon, Christian
rock music. They would hear testimonies about how Jesus
Christ had changed lives, and many found a relationship with
Him. It was the high point of the hippie era, and southern
California attracted thousands of our nation's young, restless,
and disillusioned. It was definitely the right place for such a
ministry.

During the next several years there were attempts to establish coffee houses in every town in California. Many failed. Take the town of Santa Clarita, for instance. Its population is 6,900. The main industry is citrus farming. Downtown Santa Clarita consists of two blocks of store buildings. The young people of Santa Clarita travel twenty miles to the coast if they want to go to the movies or bowling or skating or to have pizza—even to find a McDonald's. When a coffee house was opened in 1973, it never really "got off the ground." Why? By 7:00 P.M. every store and business in town was closed. Main Street was deserted. The few likely prospects had all gone to the coast to find something to do. It was definitely the wrong place.

2. *The right time.* Betty organized a study for young women in our community. She saw a need for young mothers to get together for teaching and support on how to be a successful Christian wife and mother in today's world. Betty carefully planned a course. She selected a time and place for the meetings. She plotted each session and lined up speakers and programs. She got out the publicity to every conceivable place. Women were personally invited. When the day of the first meeting arrived, no one came. After three weeks with no attendance, she dropped the whole project. It was a good idea. There certainly seemed to be a need. Perhaps June 4 was not the right time to begin.

3. *The right attitude.* Why is it you want to accomplish this task or ministry? What is the motive that keeps driving you on?

I sat across the desk from a young successful manufacturing executive. I had just presented him with a challenge. I wanted him to accept the position of Sunday school superintendent of our church. The offer was challenging because it is one of the most time demanding and important jobs in our church. I was excited to learn that Charley accepted.

I had carried out the principles for choosing people to minister with you as mentioned in chapter 7, "Ministry Partners." I looked for the very best person for the job, regardless of how busy he might presently be. He had spent over two months considering the position.

My happiness about the situation stemmed from two things. For one thing, Charley had the visible signs of the kinds of gifts and talents needed for this ministry. He was well-equipped to organize, administrate, and motivate. He was a goal setter and a goal achiever. He was the kind that got things done. Underlying all this was his commitment to Christ and his desire to do God's will.

The thing that made me rejoice the most, however, was that he was hesitant about the position because he was not sure he could handle it. He sincerely believed the job was over his head. I told him I was glad that he was honest and I was sure that he was right. The job was over his head. What Christian could think he had the wisdom and power of himself to chart out the spiritual education of hundreds of people? It is an overwhelming responsibility.

"There's only one way I can do it," Charley said. "I'll have to throw myself on the continuing grace and mercy of the Lord. If He doesn't help me, there's no way I can succeed."

That is what made me happiest. Charley had the right attitude.

Look again at what Jesus says in Mark 10:27: "All things are possible with God." In Mark 9:23 He says, "All things are possible to him who believes."

Let that sink in. Do you hear what He is saying? Do you really understand what that means for your ministry? That means God and you can run the Sunday school department. It means God and you can have a spiritual impact on the high school campus. It means God and you can begin a new church work in the poor part of town. It means God and you can start a Bible school in South America. It means God and you can start a whole new missionary movement. It means God and you can build that needed hospital for native Americans on the reservation. It means God and you can even convert your mother-in-law. God and you can do anything.

Great things for the Lord cannot be done from puny ideas. You must throw off your feeble human schemes and start dreaming God's dreams. What kind of thing would He like to do in your life? In the life of your family? In the life of your church? In the life of your community? In the life of your world? Do not hold back. Go all out. Shoot for the moon, you and the Lord. You and the Lord can go a lot farther than the moon.

How can you accomplish the impossible?

1. Write down what you would like to see done for the Lord in your family, town, church, and so on. It does not matter how much time, talent, money, or faith it will take. Dream big.

2. Take it to the Lord. Ask Him to show you if there is any reason why that would not be according to His will. Search the Scriptures and pray. Give the idea time to grow or wither.

3. Check it out with other Christians. Do they think the project is needed? Do they think it would glorify God? Do they think it is beyond mere human strength?

4. Can you visualize doing this by using only your own ingenuity, skills, and wisdom? Does it seem beyond your accomplishments?

5. Are you willing to spend hours in striving prayer, casting yourself at His feet, learning to rely totally on Him for the success of this project?

6. Get going! On a large sheet of paper write, "God and I are going to ———————————————————————"

Keep this sign in front of you. Put it on your office wall (yes, in front of everyone), or tape it to your television, or hang it on the refrigerator, or tack it on the ceiling of your bedroom (where you will see it first thing in the morning), or place it inside the cover of your Bible, or on your desk. Begin to plan, plot, and promote this idea or ministry. Write on your sign the day's date. That is the official groundbreaking of your impossible task that the Lord and you are going to do.

Many Christians have mediocre success because they have tackled only mediocre ideas. That is not to say that we all have many mundane and common tasks that we should suddenly discard. Indeed, we cannot. We must complete them and complete them *well*. The true joy of spiritual accomplishment will come only as we reach out beyond our own possibilities and grab hold of impossibilities that only God can do through us.

12

Superprayer

All Christians pray. Even if it is only the silent prayer before the pastoral prayer, even if it is merely grace before meals, even if it is a desperate crisis prayer when suddenly faced with an overwhelming catastrophe, all Christians pray.

Some Christians pray more than others. Some folks have more time, more energy, more discipline, or more commitment. The truth is, they just spend more hours in direct communication with the Father. Maybe it is the pastor. Maybe it is the Thursday morning Bible study leader. Maybe it is your saintly father. All of us know someone who outdoes us in the prayer department.

All Christians pray. All Christians should pray more. I do not need to convince you of that. You have felt guilty about it for years. And there is probably little help for you on that point. If you have been struggling with developing a consistent prayer life, you might as well know that the struggle will go on and on and on. Satan knows that prayer is much too important, too vital, too powerful an exercise to let go unhindered. He will attack, distract, and try to negate every prayer you make between now and his final departure into the lake of fire.

Struggling with prayer is your proof of its importance. Keep pushing, keep struggling, keep praying. Your diligence will bring multiplied blessings.

There is an area in your prayer life that you can improve right now. It has to do with quality, not quantity. I call it superprayer. Maybe you cannot find more time, but you can discover a few things to help you put more into it.

Some folks rebel at the thought that there is anything that needs to be taught about prayer.

"Isn't that each man's private affair with God?" "That is no secret. Anyone can do it." "Even little children know how."

"It's just one of those things that happens naturally when you become a Christian. Right?"

Yes and no.

Certainly anyone can pray. God has created us so that any person, in whatever circumstance or situation, is able to pray the sinner's prayer: "Lord, have mercy upon me. Save me from my sins."

Little children can do it. Senior citizens can do it. Even presidents of countries can do it. However, that is not all there is to a prayer life. A person who has been a Christian for fifty years is expected to progress beyond, "Now I lay me down to sleep . . ." If he does not, his Christian growth seems stunted. Our prayer lives must mature and develop. Prayer (beyond the sinner's confession) is a learned skill.

The disciples had to learn how to pray. "Lord, teach us to pray," they said (Luke 11:1). They did not ask at that point for instruction about teaching, preaching, or healing. Their hearts longed for more meaningful prayer.

For those who hold to the foolish notion that prayer will just naturally happen, answer this: What in life can we do *naturally* and please God? By *nature* man is evil, selfish, bitter, immoral, greedy, "desperately wicked." Giving in to those natural impulses produces rebellion against God. We are not called to do whatever comes naturally, but rather what comes supernaturally. We do not want natural prayer warriors, but supernatural prayer warriors, using superprayer.

What is superprayer? The disciples found out (Mark 11:20-26). It is a fascinating account. When His followers asked Jesus about His motive, He ignored their question and showed them His method instead. The background of this account is so bizarre that this story stands out completely unique among all Jesus' miracles.

It all began when Jesus and His disciples came upon a fig

tree on their way from Bethany to Jerusalem. Jesus was hungry, so when they approached the fig tree He examined it for fruit. There was none. Verse 13 explains, "It was not the season for figs."

Then comes the shocker. Jesus cursed that individual tree: "May no one ever eat fruit from you again!" Then, they continued on their way to Jerusalem.

The following day they passed the same fig tree. The disciples were stunned. The tree was dead, completely withered from the roots up. The first question that came to their minds was the same one that comes to you and me two thousand years later: Why did Jesus curse a fig tree that was not even in season?

Jesus never answered that question. Let us be satisfied that the fruitless tree was sacrificed to teach us a lesson about God's power, much the same as the destruction of two thousand swine in Mark 5. A fervent search for His motive sidetracks us from what He wants to tell us. This passage has a deep lesson in superprayer. If we miss that, we miss the whole point.

Jesus tells the disciples that there are five things they need to do in order to have a superprayer prayer life.

1. *Have faith in God.* Those words mean more than believing in Jesus Christ as Lord and Savior. Jesus is not discussing salvation, but prayer. A major factor for so many puny praying Christians is that they really do not have much faith in the God they are praying to. They have enough for salvation, but do they have enough to wilt a fig tree?

Faith in God means believing God is going to do all He said He would do. Peter had a lot of faith. He had seen Jesus do miracles for three years. Yet, when confronted with the dead fig tree, he was startled. He really was surprised that it happened. Jesus said, in effect, "Peter, if you had faith in Me, that is, believed that I'm going to do all I say, you wouldn't be surprised to find this tree dead."

Peter's problem was the same as ours. He had a hard time with this miracle because it did not fit previously established categories. He knew Jesus could heal, deliver, multiply loaves, and walk on water. But curse a fig tree? It did not seem to fit.

We, like Peter, limit God by our preconceptions. We limit Him
to our own meager categories. We try to tame C. S. Lewis's
Aslan.

Edenville Church was dying. The ethnic group that founded
the church in the tiny rural California village had become pros-
perous and moved into the city. No one of that culture was
left to attend and support the church. All available housing in
town was filled by a new and completely different cultural
group. Attempts were repeatedly made to incorporate both cul-
tures into one church. They failed miserably.

"It is impossible to reach this new group," the Christians
said.

"It is impossible," the denomination said.

"It is impossible," the community said.

"No, it will work. I have faith in God," said Mario.

Who is Mario? A superprayer, that's who. When absolutely
no one would take the responsibility of church leadership because of the impossibility of the task, Mario said, "I believe
God can do it." Did He? Yes!

It took the complete death of the old church, the rebirth
of a new bilingual church, Mario's visiting every home several
times, and three long years of much prayer and little fruit.
Finally, the efforts paid off. God miraculously established a
church in a hard-to-reach cultural setting. The Kingdom of
God blossomed in Edenville.

2. *Ask in clear, concrete terms.* Jesus did not curse everything in sight—not plant life in general, nor every fig tree, but
rather one individual, specific tree. He did not pray for "bad
things" to happen to it. He asked that it would never produce
fruit again. There was only one way that curse could be proved.
The tree must die. It must die right then. It did.

"Say to *this* mountain, be *taken up* and *cast* into *the sea*"
(Mark 11:23, italics added).

There was only one way that request could be granted. The
mountain which was being pointed out would have to rise up
like a cloud, rush headlong toward the sea, and plunge beneath
the foamy brine. Anything else would not really be the answer.

We may never have the need for casting mountains into the sea, but we must all discover that it is His will that we pray in specific terms, clearly stating what it is we are asking Him to do.

There are several reasons we talk to God in ambiguous terms. First, we are not always sure what we want. That might suffice in those emergency times when we are suddenly brought to our knees by the situation at hand. But this is certainly the exception. Most of the time our prayers come after much contemplation. We consider things for a long time. During this time we must continually ask ourselves, what exactly do I want God to do in this situation? How will I know when He has done it?

Suppose you have been asked to pray during the week of your church's daily vacation Bible school. You could spend time each day praying for God to "bless," "use," "inspire," and so forth. What is it you are really asking God to do? How will you know when He has answered those prayers?

On the other hand, suppose you spent the same amount of time each day with requests like these, "Lord, give Carrie, who teaches the second grade, strength in her back so she won't need to drop out before the week is through. Give Tommie in kindergarten a calm week so he will stop picking on Melissa. We need twenty dozen cookies by ten, Tuesday morning. Help Joy have time to individually present the way of salvation to each of the fifth graders. Bring out at least fifty percent of the parents for the closing rally on Friday night."

That does not mean, of course, that God is forced to answer every prayer exactly as you asked. But He *will* answer, and both He and you will know exactly what you are asking for. That kind of prayer takes some preparation. You must know the program, situation, and people involved. That extra preparation is what it takes to turn ordinary prayer into superprayer.

There is a second reason we hesitate to pray in concrete terms. Sometimes our motives are not altogether pure. We are a little ashamed to have Him search our hearts in the matter. That shows itself in several ways.

I might, for example, pray for God to "bless" my church. That is hard to measure. It is unclear what I really expect God to do. On the other hand, I could ask God to bring 20 percent of the people in the new subdivision into our church fellowship. But, I do not pray that because I know the reason I want them to come to our church is so that *my* church might be the fastest growing in town, so that *my* church might have more prestige, so that *my* church will have added income. I do not want the Lord to see all that so I just say, "Lord, bless our church." It is not wrong for me to pray about specific growth in our church, but I must be willing to let the Lord scrutinize and deal with my motives.

Another reason we do not pray specifically is that sometimes we do not mean our prayers at all. If we can couch the requests in abstract phrases and meaningless, measureless terms, then we foolishly assume our insincerity will not be discovered.

Suppose that two hundred workers suddenly lost their jobs when new owners took over the factory in your part of town. They are going to automate and will not need the workers. It happens that your home is located right at the edge of the tract of homes where most of the workers live. For the past several months you have had a running battle with your neighbors who have misused your property, badgered your children, run down the neighborhood, and kept you awake at night with their noise. Harry, next door, happens to be one of those laid off. It looks as though Harry and his family will be moving to another town to look for employment.

On the Sunday after the firing, you go to church to find there is great community sympathy for the jobless. Your preacher has the nerve to ask that each one present agree to spend time during the week praying for those needing to find jobs. You will probably pray something like this, "Lord, help all those who lost their jobs. Amen." What you should be praying is, "Lord, guide Harry to a new job that will meet the economic necessities of his family. Help him find a job before the unemployment checks run out in October. And, please, Lord, help him find a job here in this city because you know his wife, Marci, needs to live close to her elderly mother."

You will not pray that way, of course, because you have a personal stake in the matter. You do not really want Harry and his family to remain your neighbors. Until you deal with your motives, you will not ask anything specific from God, and you will remain the poorer for it.

3. *Rid yourself of doubts.* The first doubt we most often need to confront is, Is it really God's will? In the midst of a faith-stretching prayer request the words of 1 John 5:14-15 slip into our minds: "And this is the confidence which we have before Him, that, if we ask anything according to His will, He hears us. And if we know that He hears us in whatever we ask, we know that we have the requests which we have asked from Him."

Is this request of mine really His will? How can I know for sure? Is it possible to know? On and on the questions come until the doubts have drowned any hope of faith.

Although it is true that "God's ways are above our ways," and there are always mysteries of the faith that we cannot completely understand, *God's will is knowable.* The Bible overflows with God's will. Just about any page will tell you plainly what He wills.

It is not God's will that any should perish (2 Peter 3:9). It is not God's will that believers continue in sin (1 John 2:1). It is God's will that every person hear the gospel (Mark 16:15). It is God's will that Christians live in peace and joy (John 16:33). It is not God's will for His children to live defeated lives (Romans 8:31-39). It is not God's will that you misuse His miraculous power in order to bring glory to yourself (Acts 8:9-25). God's will is knowable, if you take time to read His Word. For the most part you can know His will before you ever go to Him with your prayer need.

Another doubt that often plagues our prayers is, Do I really want this to happen? It is not difficult to allow your prayer life to slip into a habitual ritual. Just how badly do you want this to happen? Bad enough to spend hours in prayer if need be? Bad enough to dedicate your life to its completion? The quality of your prayer improves when your heart sincerely longs for the answer.

Sometimes the doubt hampering us is, Is this God's method? We might be convinced thoroughly that God wants us to build a church in a certain city, but does He want us to cast the Auto Wrecking and Junk Yard into the sea in order to secure the needed property? Unfortunately, the Bible does not list every conceivable acceptable method. But we do know a few things. God's methods are never immoral. They are not self-glorifying. They must sincerely help to meet the needs of people. They either build up His Kingdom, tear down the works of Satan, or both.

Armed with a godly method and a knowledge of God's will, take your request to the Lord with all your heart. You will find your prayer life brimming with vitality.

4. *Believe it is going to happen before it does.* Does that seem impossible? Jesus said, "Therefore I say to you, all things for which you pray and ask, believe that you have received them, and they shall be granted you" (Mark 11:24).

The word for this phenomenon—that is, believing you are going to receive something before you see it—is faith. That is what the Christian life is all about. That is what separates the men from the boys, so to speak. "Now faith is the assurance of things hoped for, the conviction of things not seen" (Hebrews 11:1). The "heroes of the faith" in Hebrews 11 were heroes because they all used that principle. They believed before they actually saw. How does that look in everyday living?

Suppose you went down to the department store and purchased a washing machine. You told the clerk exactly what you needed, and he helped you select just the right one for you. As you pay for it the clerk tells you, "Your machine will be delivered and installed next Tuesday morning."

Now what do you do? Sometime before next Tuesday you will move the old washer, clean out the lint and debris hiding behind it, and perhaps purchase some new fittings for the faucet that is starting to crack. When Tuesday morning arrives, you have everything in the laundry room ready for your new washer. You acted by faith, believing the machine would be delivered before it actually came.

The same goes for your prayer life. You bring to the Lord a reasonable request. As far as you can determine it is according to His will and His methods. You desire for it to happen, and you believe God can do it. Now it is time to leave the situation with Him and prepare things in readiness for His answer.

Perhaps you have asked for an opportunity to share your faith with a colleague at work. Now get busy brushing up on the basic elements of bringing someone to the Lord. You have asked that the neighbors attend church with you. Now go out and clean up the backseat of the car. You have asked that your children might attend a good Christian college. Now go down and open that savings account for them.

5. *Don't forget the forgiveness disclaimer.* At the conclusion of Jesus' teaching about superprayer, He adds what seems to be a mere aside, "And whenever you stand praying, forgive, if you have anything against anyone; so that your Father also who is in heaven may forgive you your transgressions" (Mark 11: 25).

I call that a disclaimer because it seems Jesus is saying, "All of the above is null and void if you come to Me with unforgiveness in your heart toward others." Our prayers are drastically affected by our relationships with others. Peter mentions the same idea in 1 Peter 3:7, when he reminds husbands that if they are mistreating their wives, God will not listen to their prayers. It is also explained in Matthew 5:23-24. Jesus says there that your worship of God is pointless if your relationships with others are out of order.

Superprayer Worksheet

1. Have faith in God. Can you honestly say that you believe God can give you an answer to this request, even if you have never seen Him answer this way before?

2. <u>Ask in clear, concrete terms.</u> Write out in clear, legible, grammatical sentences exactly what it is you are asking God to do. Spend some time meditating on your true motives.

3. <u>Rid yourself of doubts.</u>
   a) How do I know this is really God's will?
   b) Does my heart really long for this answer?
   c) Does it seem to be a godly method?

4. <u>Believe it is going to happen before it does.</u> If God answers this prayer exactly as you have asked, what will you need to do in the meantime?

   a)

   b)

   c)

   Are you truly prepared for the answer?

5. <u>Do not forget the forgiveness disclaimer.</u> Every time I hear Jesus say, "Forgive," whose name keeps coming to mind?

   Do I want this prayer answer enough to humble myself and make this situation right?

13

Bargain Price Fame

Eternal praise and admiration for two measly mites—what a bargain! It was, of course, the widow's attitude rather than her money that made her the heroine of the day. Yet she did receive a lot of fame for only a couple of coins.

Midway between Palm Sunday and Good Friday we find Jesus and His followers in the Temple of Jerusalem. Often His time was spent in teaching and dialogue. This one time, however, He just sat down and did some people-watching. The startling thing was the particular people Jesus chose to watch. He sat down next to the treasury to see how much money people were bringing to the Temple (Mark 12:41-44).

How unusual, we think, for Jesus to pry into such a personal matter. Most modern-day Christians would be angered if someone leaned over their shoulders to examine the contents of their offering. In fact, living in the age of offering envelopes and personal checks, we can effectively discourage anyone's knowing what we give to the Lord's work.

That was not true in the first century. Then, perhaps as now, people related the size of the offering to the sincerity of the heart. The bigger the offering, the holier the giver. Those who really wanted to impress others would hire trumpeters to go before them, to better call attention to the fact that a large contribution was about to be made. Others were a little more subtle.

The large clay urn that served as an offering container was located where you could make your giving a public act. The large pottery could make a loud ringing sound if the coins were dropped with sufficient velocity and quantity. It did not take people long to learn how to get the loudest sounds.

As Jesus watched that ritual, many rich persons made huge offerings. Even if they were unaware of who He was, I am sure it was gratifying to have someone so intently watching their giving. After such ostentatious displays, a widow approached. Jesus carefully watched her too. The coins she dropped were worth less than a cent. No doubt she would not have been anxious to have anyone noting that publicly. But that is exactly what Jesus did. He stopped her and pointed out to all what she did. "Truly I say to you, this poor widow put in more than all the contributors to the treasury; for they all put in out of their surplus, but she, out of her poverty, put in all she owned, all she had to live on" (Mark 12:43-44). Here Jesus taught His followers the essential ingredient of giving.

The widow loved God so much that she willingly gave all she had to His work. To her that was more important even than her daily bread. Jesus did not prevent her. He did not tell her to keep her money for she needed it. Certainly God would not have minded if instead she had purchased bread for her evening meal. To her it was important to give, and she did.

Obviously, it is not the amount we give, but the percentage. Attitude is of prime importance. Giving out of love, beyond her means, trusting God to provide, that was the woman's style. That is "Necessity Fund" giving.

Today, as in the widow's day, money is the hardest thing in the world for humans to part with. Most of us have categories of items on which we spend our money. For some, spending is carefully spelled out in the way of a monthly budget. Others keep an accounting in their heads. Either way the result is the same. It usually looks something like this:

Necessity Fund	Desirability Fund	Extra
groceries	boat payment	charities
house payment	entertainment	church
or rent	cable television	et cetera
car payment	vacation	
taxes	patio cover	
clothing	landscape yard	
doctors	new furniture	
utilities	et cetera	
et cetera		

The usual process is to take the monthly paycheck and purchase those items in the "Necessity Fund" list, then those in the
"Desirability Fund" list, and, finally, if there is some left over,
the "Extra" list is taken care of. It was out of the *"Bare* Necessity Fund" that the widow gave her last two coins.

No wonder Jesus was not impressed with the rich men's offerings. They gave out of their "Extra." Anybody can do that.
It is not much strain to give money when you really cannot
think of anything to use it for, anyway. The widow sets the
pace for all of us. The light of her gift is a beacon calling us
back to the narrow path of true discipleship whenever we are
caught in the materialism of our day.

This should, perhaps, be the first chapter of the book. If
anyone is not willing to face the issue of money and material
possessions, giving even out of the necessity fund, giving until
it hurts, then he really does not want to find true spiritual greatness, that is, success with a purpose. There are five main reasons why giving stands in the way of many people. In order to
justify their lack of solid monetary commitment to the Lord,
at least in their own minds, one of the following excuses is usually given.

1. *"I can't afford it."* This is supposed to be self-explanatory,
with no further statement needed. It is not. The only person
who truly cannot afford to give to the Lord is the one who re-

ceives absolutely nothing, either in coin or kind. The newborn baby is just about the only one in our present society that fits that category. You can afford it because God only wants a portion of what He gives in return.

To say and mean, "I can't afford it," is saying to God that He has done such a poor job of providing for you that you are worse off than the widow and, therefore, exempt from giving. The truth of the matter is, you cannot afford not to give.

2. *"I give my share."* This age-old excuse surfaces in two ways. First, there is the notion that as long as I give something every time I go to church or a meeting, I have given *my share*. There is a certain self-gratification in reaching into your purse or wallet each time the offering plate is passed and pulling out a bill (usually the smallest, of course). Is *your share* merely what you have in petty cash?

Another way we use this excuse is to figure that if everyone gave the way we do, then the church, mission group, or whatever would be in good financial condition. We think that makes good sense. If every member gave $200 a year (as you do), then the budget would be met. Even if we could blindly overlook the fact that some members have little income, some live out of town and have discontinued giving, and many stopped giving when they stopped coming, our logic would still be wrong. Our giving to the Lord has nothing to do with what others give. God is not interested in comparison, but in proportion. Jesus is still sitting by the offering container watching our giving. He sees not only how much we put in, but how much we hold back.

3. *"I don't know how the money will be spent."* What if it is misused? What if it is squandered away? What if it is spent on something I do not like?

The problem with such logic is that you are not even considering that you are giving first and foremost to the Lord. Once you give it to Him, it is His money. It is not up to you to be responsible for how every penny is spent. That is not to imply, of course, that we should not be discerning. But, the widow certainly did not hold back her two coins in fear that it might be used to help purchase a new couch for the Temple guards' lounge. You have not been appointed executor of the Lord's estate. The total worth of your gift has more to do with the trust and faith in your heart than the amount on the check and what it happens to be used for.

4. *"I don't like the preacher (teacher, missionary, etc.)."* It is quite common to hear such a statement from an otherwise faithful disciple of the Lord. This is the idea that the most effective way to voice our disapproval of how things are being run is to withhold our funds. The best way to get rid of the pastor is to stop giving to the church. This approach might be correct if (1) the pastor were a Hollywood celebrity competing in a popularity contest, or (2) it were the preacher's church. Neither is true. No matter who stands behind the pulpit on Sunday mornings, it is the church of Jesus Christ. The pastor did not "win" the position; it was assigned to him by the Lord Himself.

The point is: We are to give to God. Most of the time our dissatisfaction with the personnel is just a convenient excuse to keep more money for ourselves. There are plenty of other channels to use to voice our sincere reservations about another's ministry.

5. *"I'll make it up later."* If all else fails, this excuse is always handy. We think that since the important thing is giving, not when we give, we will spend a little more on ourselves this month and make it up later. I do not need to tell you what happens in actuality when this faulty logic is carried to completion. The Lord gets shortchanged.

We begin to realize why giving is the hardest of all concepts. It hurts to talk about our giving habits. We have a difficult time parting with the security, power, and prestige of money. The Lord knew we would. That is why He made it a prerequisite for discipleship.

He also knows we need help in carrying out such a difficult assignment. You have heard for years about "tithes and offerings," the giving of 10 percent and additional for special concerns. Some people teach that the really spiritual person will give a double tithe, or 20 percent. How much does the Lord demand? How should we figure our tithe? On gross income? Or take-home pay? There must be as many different ways of figuring giving as there are stewardship committees. There is a little known secret that can assist the sincere follower.

The secret is to give God 100 percent of all the money you make. Give God everything. That includes the paycheck, the retirement fund, the social security, the savings accounts, the college fund, the money from the garage sale, the birthday check from Aunt Dorothy, the refund on the coupons, everything. Does that sound radical? You had better believe it. Remember, this is a book about radical discipleship.

Now, you say, if I give everything to God, my family and I ought to make it about two weeks before we starve to death. Wait. Once you have gathered up every account, fund, and source of income and in prayer sincerely have given it all to God, then go to Him and ask for an allowance. He certainly knows what you need to live on. He wants to provide those needs. The way to figure your possible allowance is to divide your budget into necessities, desirabilities, and extras. Take your necessities list to the Lord. Ask Him to convict you or affirm you on any of the items. Ask Him for the amount of money needed for the revised list.

The rest of the income belongs to the Lord. You do not even need to bother trying to figure if you should give it to Him or not. It is already His.

Note several things. First, your "allowance" is set between you and the Lord. Nobody tells you what that should be. Nobody judges you for what result you have decided upon. Neither can you judge nor enforce your necessities list on anyone else. We are all different and have differing needs.

Second, such an outlook on your finances does not mean you will spend your life barely surviving. Jesus did promise us an abundant life. If we accept the necessity allowance and do not plot and scheme for the luxuries, we will find that God will (often miraculously) provide many of the desirabilities, anyway. He will fill our lives to the brim with contentment and include many of the items we considered as extras. By refusing to focus our concern on those items, we give Him an opportunity to provide them for us in His own special way.

Third, there are many in this world who do not have much more than the necessity allowance. Perhaps you find in all honesty that you actually need more income to meet even the necessities. If that is your situation, then figure the amount you will need to meet those necessities (right down to the dollar and cents) and ask Him to provide that amount. Then watch Him provide.

That, of course, is extreme. Most of us would be quite embarrassed to have the Lord closely scrutinize our "necessities" list. It may be more padded than pork barrel legislation in Congress.

A final reminder—the widow's small coins came out of her necessity fund. God may, at times, want you to give even out of your necessities. Do not hold back. Jesus calls us to a radical commitment in giving; not only that we can prove our love and obedience to Him, but also that we can experience the full blessings of God. For it is only for such givers that the "windows of heaven" are opened (see Malachi 3:10). You will never achieve true spiritual greatness until you are free from the enslaving power of money.

Financial Worksheet

1. Determine your total family income. (Easy to secure from your tax forms.)

   a) $_____.

   b) Give every penny of this sum to the Lord. Let Him know that as far as you are concerned, it belongs to Him. If none is given back to you, you will not complain (see Job 1:21 for proper attitude).

2. Develop a Necessity Fund budget. Determine the amount
   you need to meet these items.

   a) Food (Reexamine that gro-
       cery bill. Non-food items
       do not count, nor do gour-
       met items.) $_____ per month

   b) Lodging (House pay-
       ment, taxes, rent, insur-
       ance, upkeep, etc. Could
       it possibly be you are
       overhoused?) $_____ per month

   c) Clothing (Remember: Ne-
       cessities.) $_____ per month

   d) Transportation (Include
       payments, upkeep, gas,
       etc. Is the Lord con-
       vinced you need more
       than one car?) $_____ per month

   e) Medical $_____ per month

   f) Other $_____ per month

   g) Other $_____ per month

   h) Other $_____ per month

                                      $_____ Total

3. If your income list exceeds your necessity list, all of the
   difference should go to the Lord's work. It is His because
   (a) you gave Him everything, and (b) He provided you
   with an income in excess of needs. If your income barely
   meets or fails to meet your necessity list, cut back from
   each category and, like the widow, give the leftover to
   the Lord.

4. Now in careful prayer let the Lord examine what you
   have done. Tell Him the details of each item. See if He
   agrees with your reasoning. Let Him readjust the list

if He wants to. Do not play games with Him. Do not think you can hide items by purposely leaving them off your list.

All of that is time consuming and difficult to carry out. You did not expect greatness—success with a purpose—to come easy, did you? Try it. He will not fail you.

14

Avoiding Dead-end Streets

Many an otherwise successful ministry has had its effectiveness minimized, even canceled completely, by running down dead-end streets. The more spiritual sounding the name of the street, the more workers it snares.

Take, for instance, the street named "prophecy." It is, in its purest form, one of the important elements of our belief. Not only the prophecy that has already been fulfilled but also the sure and certain signs of what is to come are central to true Christian doctrine. Many souls wander for years among the garbage cans of this wayside trap they mistakenly thought was prophecy. Not all that is called prophetic is actually biblical prophecy. One of Satan's effective tools is to lead Christians down fruitless paths of false prophecy. That is almost a universal characteristic of a cult.

Pacific Christian Chapel was the only church in the town of Gold Coast that made any effort to reach the thousands of tourists that flocked to the small seaside resort each summer. The off-season population of Gold Coast was eighteen hundred. But, in the summer as many as ten thousand people crowded the state park, the resort motels, and the beaches. The other three churches in town were content to minister to the steady residents and pick up an occasional visitor. Not so for Pacific Chapel.

The Chapel sponsored Christian concerts every Friday night on the beach. They spent weekends reaching out to the vacationers with well-trained witnessing teams. The state park officials allowed them to hold early morning Sunday services for the campers. Sometimes they moved their whole Sunday morning service out to the amphitheater next to the pier and were able to reach hundreds more than normal.

Every penny of increased income funded help for stranded tourists and transients who paraded continuously through town. That was quite a ministry for a church of only 150 members.

However, today there is no tourist ministry in Gold Coast. The white church building that once was Pacific Christian Chapel is painted violet and says, "Sandy's Surf Stuff." What happened?

In 1974 the pastor of Pacific Chapel felt convinced that the Lord had revealed to him through Scriptures that these were the last days. And in these last days there would be terrible earthquakes, especially on the West Coast. He believed the Lord was warning him that a great earthquake would soon happen in Gold Coast and that he and his church should move to another location.

In August of 1974, twenty-four families (the core group of the church) moved to Two Rivers, Montana. They sold the church property, sold their homes, and purchased a ranch there in western Montana.

In Montana the little band of worshipers kept mostly to themselves, trying to establish an economic base to support themselves. Within a few months, the number of families dwindled. By 1977 only eight families were left, the farm was greatly in debt, and they had no impact on the surrounding community. Finally, in the winter of 1978-79 the group disbanded, sold the ranch, and went their separate ways. Meanwhile, back in Gold Coast tourists still come and go, most unaware of what they are missing. The people of Pacific Christian Chapel were sincere Christians who got sidetracked.

Wally had the best bus ministry in town. Every Saturday you would see him canvass the neighborhood, calling on prospective riders. Without fail his familiar blue bus could be seen stopping at dozens of Cypress View homes every Sunday. He brought many to Sunday school and then delivered them back home again. He would sing with them, joke with them, and tell them about Jesus. Some Saturdays he would load them into the bus and take them all for a picnic or down to the city for a Dodgers baseball game.

Wally does not have time to drive the bus anymore. He is too busy studying. He took a course in biblical prophecy last fall at the nearby Bible college and was a little disappointed. He thought they should have more answers. He was convinced that he could dig out and discover the modern fulfillment of many biblical prophecies. For the past several months Wally has spent every free moment in libraries, studying at home, poring over every piece of literature he can find to complete his prophetic chart. There is hardly a book or pamphlet on the subject he has not read. I have not talked to Wally in some time. The last I knew he was working to prove that the recognition of Red China was the direct fulfillment of 1 Chronicles 26:18. I think about him often—especially every Sunday morning when I pass his church and see the blue bus sitting idly by.

Prophecy can, like other dead-end streets, lead you into spiritual ineffectiveness. Misuse of prophecy can also lead to spiritual error, a more serious mistake, which can cripple any disciple. If he can, Satan will not only distract you, he will try to permanently disable you. Myriads of cultic groups line the Christian trail to waylay any they can who travel down the path of discipleship. The arrows they shoot are often "false prophecy" in disguise.

Maybe this sidetrack checklist will help:

1. Will this force you to give up any ministry that the Lord is currently blessing? Yes ( ) No ( )
    (If yes, forget it.)

2. Does it hold any hope of increasing your personal knowledge of God? Yes ( ) No ( )
    (If no, is it worth it?)

3. Is it the kind of sidetrack that could easily become a life-time involvement? Yes ( ) No ( )
    (The best way out of quicksand is to avoid it in the first place.)

4. Will your involvement help the real needs of other people? Yes ( ) No ( )
    (If no, why bother?)

Misuse of prophecy is not new. It was rampant in Jesus' day. Paul warned the early church that it would be a problem for them (see 2 Timothy 4:3-4). Jesus knew there would be plenty of false "end-time prophets," so He explained things carefully to the disciples (Mark 13). It would be a grave mistake for any serious follower of Jesus to neglect to study Mark 13 thoroughly, as well as the other prophetic passages in the Bible. There are two general principles in the Mark passage that must be grasped by anyone striving to find true spiritual success.

First, Jesus reassures His followers that they have heard the truth of the matter. "Heaven and earth will pass away, but My words will not pass away" (Mark 13:31). That is Jesus' formal seal upon the words He had just spoken. Perhaps we feel such a declaration is not needed. Are not all of Jesus' words true? Of course they are. Yet He knew some would come along with other end-time teachings. He wanted to remind us all that His words are the final authority. Heaven's and earth's existence are only temporary compared to the authority of His words.

We live in the world that claims that Jesus' teaching is no longer valid. Some say it is outdated; others say God is working in new and different ways for a new and different age. That is wrong. All of Jesus' teachings, including that about end times, is valid for all times. When we get bogged down in prophecy debates we must never forget this.

A second important principle found in Mark 13 is this: Jesus reassured His followers that He had told them everything in advance (v. 23). All the revelation they needed was given. That does not mean that Jesus told them everything in detail (such as the day or hour), but Jesus told them all they needed to know about the subject. You and I do not need any more information about end times than Jesus revealed. It is important that we try to understand all that He said. It is equally important to refuse to listen to those who would add to His revelation.

Even a casual reading through the New Testament makes one aware that just a few years after the death of Jesus, and a few months after the birth of the church at Pentecost, false teachers and prophets abounded.

> I know that after my departure savage wolves will come in among you, not sparing the flock; and from among your own selves men will arise, speaking perverse things, to draw away the disciples after them. [Acts 20:29-30]

> I am amazed that you are so quickly deserting Him who called you by the grace of Christ, for a different gospel; which is really not another; only there are some who are disturbing you, and want to distort the gospel of Christ. But even though we, or an angel from heaven, should preach to you a gospel contrary to that which we have preached to you, let him be accursed. [Galatians 1:6-8]

> If any one advocates a different doctrine, and does not agree with sound words, those of our Lord Jesus Christ, and with the doctrine conforming to godliness, he is conceited and understands nothing; but he has a morbid interest in controversial questions and disputes about words, out of which arise envy, strife, abusive language, evil suspicions, and constant friction between men of depraved mind and deprived of the truth, who suppose that godliness is a means of gain. [1 Timothy 6:3-5]

> Beloved, do not believe every spirit, but test the spirits to see whether they are from God; because many false prophets have gone out into the world. [1 John 4:1]

If the world of A.D. 50-100 was filled with false prophets, how great a crowd there must be now. What are we to do? We need a "spirit tester," something to apply to each side issue that lures us away from the main path. Consider the following.

1. *Is this teaching based on extrabiblical information?*
   Yes ( ) No ( )
   a) Are extrabiblical sources quoted? constantly ( )
      often ( )   occasionally ( )   seldom ( )
      never ( )
   b) Does the proof of the teaching depend upon how one sees current world affairs? Yes ( ) No ( )
   c) Does acceptance of this teaching mean you will have to live your life differently? Yes ( ) No ( )
      (Any teaching that has no measurable effect upon your life or the life of the one proposing it is not worth the time.)
   d) Do proponents of this teaching spend more time talking about
      the doctrine ( )   the originator of the teaching ( ) or Jesus and His teachings ( )?

2. *Does this teaching honor the deity and work of Jesus Christ?* Yes ( ) No ( )
   a) If you believe all the teaching proposes, would you tend to increase your love of God and desire to actively serve Him? Yes ( ) No ( )
   b) Is there any way this teaching makes Jesus less than the Bible reveals Him to be? For instance:
      (1) Are Jesus' words said to be incomplete and therefore new words are needed? Yes ( )
          No ( )
      (2) Is Jesus portrayed as wholly God and wholly man? Yes ( ) No ( )
   c) Jesus said that His words are entirely true and that He had revealed all things in advance. Does this teaching support that idea? Yes ( ) No ( )

3. *Could a person who had never heard of this teaching honestly be expected to discover it with nothing more than a Bible?* Yes ( ) No ( )

   a) Is this teaching held by people in different kinds of Christian work? Yes ( ) No ( )

   b) Has a similar belief been held by others in the history of the Christian church? Yes ( ) No ( )

4. *Is the prophetic teaching measurable?* Yes ( ) No ( )

   a) Is this teaching mentioned in such general terms that you would never know if it came true or not? Yes ( ) No ( )

   b) Are only a few people (i.e., leader, teacher, inner core of followers) able to properly tell when the teaching has been fulfilled? Yes ( ) No ( )

   c) Has the prophecy at any time proved to be incorrect? Yes ( ) No ( )

5. *Is the source of this teaching reliable in other matters?* Yes ( ) No ( )

   a) Do you know the proponents of this teaching personally? Yes ( ) No ( )

   b) Do they exhibit a biblical life-style? Yes ( ) No ( )

   c) Are they trustworthy in other matters in which you deal with them? Yes ( ) No ( )

   d) Do you have any reason to doubt the integrity of their faith? Yes ( ) No ( )

6. *Can this teaching pass the threefold confirmation test?*

   a) The confirmation of common sense

      (1) Does it sound right to your ears? Yes ( ) No ( )

(2) Does it seem like something God would do?
Yes ( ) No ( )

(3) Is it rational? Yes ( ) No ( )

b) The confirmation of Scriptures

(1) Is it easily supported by the Bible? Yes ( )
No ( )

(2) Is any of it based on biblical half quotes, half-
truths? Yes ( ) No ( )

(3) Does this teaching lead to biblical living?
Yes ( ) No ( )

c) The confirmation of the Spirit

(1) Does the study of this teaching bring deep spiritual peace and joy into your life? Yes ( )
No ( )

(2) Do you feel at ease around other people who
believe this way? Yes ( ) No ( )

(3) Do other people who exhibit spiritual maturity
support this teaching? Yes ( ) No ( )

All of that may seem like a considerable amount of work
to go to. It is. Yet, it is time well-spent. It takes a few minutes to check out a road map before you begin your vacation,
but it is very important that you do not spend all your hard-
earned vacation time wandering around looking for the right
road. So it is with your spiritual life.

You want to find spiritual success and greatness. You have
a fulfilling and exciting ministry ahead for the Lord. You do
not want to waste time with sidetracks that lead nowhere. Take
time to investigate any teaching or group or program that would
lead you away from the thrust of your ministry.

God has given you the tools of discernment. You need to
use them. You need not be afraid of the numerous cults and
cultic leaders. Just remember Jesus' words: "I have told you
everything in advance" (Mark 13:23).

15

What Money Can't Buy

An unnamed, uninvited woman entered Simon the leper's home, poured expensive perfume all over Jesus, and immediately secured her place of greatness in the Scriptures. The impetuous lady outdid the apostles. She succeeded in a way they never did. Why? What mysterious principle is involved here?

Mark 14 tells us it was mealtime at Simon's house. He lived in the small town of Bethany, just outside Jerusalem. Several other friends of Jesus lived nearby: Lazarus, Mary, and Martha. In fact, John 12:1-8 states that Mary did a similar act. Perhaps she is the very woman that Mark is referring to, but we will leave the woman unnamed as that is how Mark presents her.

Just to have Jesus in the house must have been a treat for Simon. Though recently healed, for some time he had not been allowed to enter the gates of a city or village. As a leper he had known much rejection and suffering as one of the despised of society. Now, he could resume a normal life and actually play host to the Master and His followers.

How disturbing it must have been to have this leisurely meal suddenly interrupted by an emotional woman. It was not a common everyday occurrence, even for Jesus. The reaction was immediate: "Such a great waste of money! Why didn't you sell this perfume and give the money to the poor instead?" protested the disciples. It was the classic "holier than thou" putdown.

They were right about the perfume's value. It was frightfully expensive, worth about a year's wages for the ordinary worker in Bethany. Yet, Jesus had a sharp word with them. "Let her

131

alone; why do you bother her? She has done a good deed to Me" (Mark 14:6).

How comforting those words must have been to the woman. We do not know all the motives behind her actions, but we do know she wanted to do something for Jesus. We can certainly empathize with that, remembering the times we have strongly desired to do something, anything, to please Him. Now people were shouting at her, angrily calling her foolish, implying that if she really loved the Lord she would have given her expensive gift to the poor.

After Jesus quieted everyone down He began to tell them about three points they needed to ponder. All were surprising to the disciples.

First, Jesus told them there will always be poor people in this world, and there will always be another chance to help them. We must see the balance in His statement. Jesus knew that because of man's sinful nature, no matter what the economic system, greed and self-centeredness would prevent the elimination of poverty. As long as there are two people on earth, one will strive to be better than the other. That does not mean we should not actively help the poor. Often money given to Jesus and His disciples was used for the needy and poor. It must always continue to be so. He assured the woman and the disciples that there are times for honoring Him with material gifts as well.

Second, He reminded them of His soon approaching death and burial. In less than forty-eight hours He would die on a cross. He saw her act as an anointing for burial.

Third, He announced that her gracious act would be a part of His eternal gospel. Wherever the gospel was preached, that story would be included.

What makes this incident so important that it will never be forgotten by the followers of Jesus? It tells us something about the pettiness of criticizing the devotion of others. There are also clues here on doing deeds of lasting value.

As a new Christian I was excited to be asked to serve on the operations committee of my home church. It was spiritually invigorating for me to be in that place of leadership in decision making. I was all set for inspiring times. How mistaken I was.

The first meeting was lengthy. A crucial issue demanded close attention. Should we accept Mrs. McDonald's offer of $500 to have the grand piano in the sanctuary refinished to match the new decor? That proposal had deep ramifications. Some of the members believed that was a poor use of the Lord's money. There were all kinds of other needs. Refugees, missionaries, and evangelistic causes needed support.

On the other hand, other members believed Mrs. McDonald should use the money as she saw fit. The money had come to her from relatives who wanted her to use it as a memorial for her recently departed parents. They had been long-time members of the church, sincere and dedicated workers who deserved the name "saints." One of their dreams had been to build a new sanctuary. They had worked hard on the project and even in their old age had been instrumental in its completion.

So now, Mrs. McDonald thought it would be honoring to the Lord and in keeping with her parents' desires to use the money to restain the piano (left from the old sanctuary).

The debate raged on and on. If you have ever served on a similar board you can believe it took 2½ hours of heated discussion. We finally agreed to let her refinish the piano, but the vote was not unanimous. I wondered at the time if we were not acting like the protesting disciples in Mark 14.

During my first year at seminary I joined the countless ranks of impoverished students. With a wife and two children to support on a part-time job, there was not much money for "extras."

Early in March, I was greeted at church by a friend who exclaimed, "What happened to your car?"

We lived next to the church and parked our car on the busy city street in front, but a brick wall prevented my seeing it from the house. We rushed out to look and found our sturdy old compact station wagon completely demolished. Later we learned that an uninsured drunk had smashed it. Our insurance did not cover his mistake, so we were left without wheels.

That was a slight inconvenience, to say the least, since school was seven miles away. With the help of a borrowed bike and rides from school friends I continued my classes. My wife and I took it all to the Lord in prayer and waited for Him to respond.

Toward the end of April, I received a phone call from a Christian friend in my hometown. A group at the church had heard of our dilemma and had taken up a collection, which they wanted us to use for a down payment on a new car. We were thrilled. We had not asked for their help, yet they had responded freely from their hearts. We woke our sons and told them the good news.

A few days later I shared that experience with my seminary classmates. Most rejoiced with me; however one did not. He was quite upset.

Why did I think the Lord had provided that money? How could I assume that I should have a car when many people in the world went to bed hungry? Couldn't that money have been used for a better cause? Was I not selfish to think only of my own material needs?

I had to think seriously about his words. Was he right? Perhaps. All I know is that my joy in the Lord's provision dimmed somewhat with guilt.

At some point we all encounter critical pettiness. Perhaps we are on the receiving end, or we could be on the giving end. We will never achieve spiritual greatness by criticizing another's means of devotion to the Lord. How can you help eliminate pettiness in your own life?

1. *Assume a sincere motive behind each action.* Too often we allow preconceptions and prejudices to control our thoughts of others.

"She couldn't be serious about wanting to do this for the Lord," we think. "Look at the way her kids act. Look at the way she runs her business. Look at how she opposed me at the annual meeting. Look at her strange ideas about the Tribulation. Look at how many worship services she's missed."

Why not assume sincere motives? Don't we expect the same? Often even an otherwise hard and callous heart can show signs of melting while offering acts of devotion to the Lord. Let the woman pour her perfume. Let Mrs. McDonald stain the piano. Let the Bly family rejoice in the Lord over their new car.

2. *Realize that every victory for the Lord is your victory too.* When the church across town has a bigger bus ministry than you do, rejoice. The Kingdom of God is spreading. When the neighbor down the street leads your own sister to the Lord, rejoice. Another name has been written in the book of life. When the missions committee votes to support someone else's choice, rejoice. The Word of the Lord will be proclaimed. When you come home from work and find your wife gave away your favorite jacket to a transient, rejoice. It was given in Jesus' name.

Paul rejoiced in other's ministries, even when he knew for a fact some were less than sincere. In Philippians he explains that he realizes some were preaching just to cause him trouble and discomfort while he was in jail. Paul says, "What then? Only that in every way, whether in pretense or in truth, Christ is proclaimed; and in this I rejoice, yes, and I will rejoice." Can we do any less?

One of the surest ways for you to find personal success is to have every Christian in town succeeding. Every victory they achieve helps to advance your Lord's position.

3. *Absolutely refuse any public criticism of another's ministry.* Nobody ever found true spiritual greatness by attacking another's work. Open criticism of another's ministry does one of two things. It could stifle any future hope that person might have of another ministry. Even though he might be wrong in what he is doing now, he might not always be wrong. You are prejudicing the people you talk to against this person, and they may never accept his ministry.

If the criticism proves false, you have not only slandered someone, but you have shown yourself to be less than reliable as a judge. Public criticism of another's means of devotion to God seldom advances His Kingdom.

Of course, there are those rare times when public criticism

is justified. Paul rightly stood up to Peter (Galatians 2:11-21). That is one of the exceptions to the rule. God has not, for the most part, chosen us to be judges of the hearts of others.

Should there be a time when you have serious doubts about the motives of others, what should you do? It is true that sin sometimes blinds us so we need someone else to tell us where changes are needed.

1. *Gather all the facts in the matter.* Get as much first-hand information as possible. If someone says, "You should see what they are doing," then go see for yourself. Take time to consider all you have discovered. Prayerfully meditate on whether there is real error involved or merely a difference of opinion or style. Just because something is not done your way, does not mean it is wrong.

2. *Privately present your information to the person involved.* Ask him if you have the facts right. Perhaps he has good explanations. If so, explain how his actions have been taken wrongly. You might suggest changes. Let him know both by your actions and words that your motive is to help him be a more successful disciple.

How impressive it would be to have been the woman who poured perfume over Jesus' head and secured a place of prominence in biblical history. None of us, of course, will find ourselves recorded in Scripture, but we can do something of lasting value. God still uses ordinary people like you and me to accomplish extraordinary results. We can learn a lot from the lady with the perfume. We will not learn exactly what to do, but we will learn what attitude pleases Him as we do it.

First, have as your chief motive love and gratefulness to the Lord. The lady was sincere in her adoration of Jesus. Nowhere do we get hints that she was purposely trying to draw attention to herself, nor do we suspect that she was purposely avoiding giving to the poor. She loved Him and brought her gift out of gratitude.

Careful consideration of our inner feelings and workings is required. Without love as a motive our deeds will burn out long before they are completed. Or we will ride the superficial high of self-praise.

Second, enter into the chosen action with reckless abandon. The lady with the alabaster vial of pure nard barged right in. Had she debated longer, she may have decided against it. What she did was certainly showy. We might even say it was brash and a bit embarrassing. Certainly it made the other guests feel uncomfortable. Yet it was right.

There are going to be times when doing the right thing may appear a bit awkward. Surely there will be times when you will feel uncomfortable. However, finding spiritual success means being a radical disciple. Radical discipleship can only be lived with reckless abandon. If you are convinced an action is what the Lord wants you to do, do not hold back. Do not spend time wondering what you will look like or what "they" will think of you. That really does not matter.

Third, focus your entire action upon the Lord. It was only after they stared at the Lord with the perfume dripping down His face that they turned to consider the lady. Any success you might have in this world would be meaningless and worthless if you are not achieving it for the Lord. He really is all there is to life. Do not waste your time on a project, cause, ministry, job, or action that is not focused on Him. Whether you lead a Girl Scout troop, teach an exercise class, translate the Scriptures into a native tongue, bake cookies, or serve as a hospital orderly, do it for His praise and glory.

Attitude Checklist

1. Why do you want this deed to succeed? Honestly list your reasons and motives.

   a)

   b)

   c)

   d)

   e)

2. If you threw yourself into this with everything you have,
    what sort of awkward situation could you anticipate?

3. Tell the Lord in prayer that you are willing to go through
    this or anything else in order for this work to succeed.

4. How can this project be done in order to give the opti-
    mum glory and praise to the Lord? List the ways.

5. "Though none go with me, yet I will follow." On

    _____(date) I will begin this ministry of

    _____, and I will hold back nothing until

    the Lord provides the success.

16

The Trouble with Fame

Most people immediately associate greatness with fame. Yet, the two are miles apart. Greatness includes achieving a high spiritual goal for the Lord. Fame only involves being known by many people. Some have accomplished great things for God without ever becoming well-known. Others are well-known without ever doing anything worthwhile for Him. And, of course, there are those few who achieve greatness and in the course of events pick up fame as well.

Jennifer Roberts is finding true greatness. Four years ago as a young mother in her early twenties she felt God wanted her to be involved in a children's ministry. It was her first experience with anything like that. She was scared, nervous, but determined. The channel for ministry proved to be a neighborhood Bible class in which she invited children in her area to her home once a week for a Bible story and games. Jennifer soon had forty five-to-twelve-year-olds. Of course, you have never heard of Jennifer Roberts. Few people will, but she is on her way to achieving true spiritual greatness.

In the fall of 1978 the world was shocked to hear the unbelievable story of over nine hundred American citizens' committing mass suicide in the South American country of Guyana. Within days Jim Jones became a household name. Jones got something he always wanted: fame. But there is nothing great about the sight of bloated corpses lying around the main pavilion of Jonestown. The combination of egomaniac and demonic forces have destroyed more lives than even the nine

hundred-plus members of the People's Temple. We can all re-
call many famous examples. Surely no one confuses those with
greatness.

The purpose of this book is to help in the striving for greatness, not fame. If fame happens to come along with the effort,
so be it. But fame is no gauge of success.

Mark 15 records the account of a famous, but not great,
person by the name of Pilate. The scene is familiar to most
everyone. Keep in mind several things. Pilate understood the
situation clearly. He knew Jesus was innocent. He knew that
it was out of envy that the religious leaders had arrested Jesus.
Pilate was not an unsuspecting simpleton who was having the
wool pulled over his eyes.

Pilate exhibited uncertainty in making sound decisions.
Armed with the facts mentioned above, he should have been
able to quickly bring justice and release Jesus. But he could
not make up his mind. As long as the trails of greatness and
fame lead side by side we have an easy path to follow. What
happens when there is a fork in the road? What happens when
we must choose between fame and greatness? For Pilate and
for us it is a hard decision.

Pilate chose fame. In verse 15 some of the most condemning
words ever written are filed against him: "And wishing to satisfy the multitude . . ." Satisfying the crowd has kept thousands
of otherwise faithful disciples from achieving greatness.

How does one choose greatness over fame?

1. *Carefully gather all the facts.* When we are caught up in
the glamour of the possibility of fame, it is common to overlook
many bits of information that would be helpful in making right
choices. Jesus says in Matthew 18:16 that we should be so
sure of a situation that "by the mouth of two or three witnesses
every fact may be confirmed." We must listen to the crowd
but investigate on our own. It is important to be able to separate commentary and personal opinion from what the true
facts might be. That is standard procedure for anyone in leadership. Pilate knew that and he tried to carry it out. The leaders were questioned. He listened to each accusation. The de-

fendant was given a chance to speak His mind. Pilate carried out that first step better than many often do.

Frank and Marsha, Bob and Sheila all became Christians about the same time. Both couples were in their late twenties and excited about their newfound faith. During their Tuesday evening home Bible study they discovered the subject of spiritual gifts and ministries. For the first time they were challenged to think what their ministry for the Lord might be. One night the topic of conversation centered on music. All four were gifted vocally and instrumentally.

They did what few people do. They told their pastor they thought their gifts might be in music and offered their services. He immediately asked them to sing for the following Sunday evening worship. Their ministry proved to be inspiring and warmly received. They sang and played often after that, and soon the pastor asked them to be in charge of music for all the Sunday night services. Attendance grew. It was a growing and vital ministry. One day they came to the crossroads. More and more people told them they should sing professionally, go on tour, and widen their ministry. That excited the four. After all, wasn't that what it meant to give up everything and follow Jesus?

Someone offered to act as their manager, and that was the sign from the Lord they had been waiting for. Bob and Frank quit their jobs, borrowed money on their homes for more deluxe equipment, and began lining up engagements. During the next several months, they found out several things. There was a lot of really good Christian musical talent around, and the competition was tough. Also, many people who were eager to have them come were unable even to pay them expenses. It is easy to substitute professionalism for devotion and allow the Lord's part in the use of gifts to slip into a subordinate position. After less than six months in that venture they felt like failures. They had not taken time to gather the facts—to count the cost before they went "all out."

The four are back at their home church now and maybe one of these days they will recover from their disappointment

enough to pick up their leadership role in music ministry there
again.

2. *Let other people involved confirm the information you
have gathered.* In Acts 5 when Ananias's deception had been
uncovered, Peter confronted Sapphira and asked her to confirm her husband's story. No decision was made concerning
Sapphira's guilt until she had a chance to confirm or deny the
facts.

We saw Pilate at least attempting to fulfill this principle.
He came to Jesus and asked him directly if the charges against
Him were true.

If Bob and Sheila and Frank and Marsha had spent some
time writing those in the music business and perhaps inter-
viewing some who successfully serve that way, they would
have been more prepared.

Recently I accepted an appointment to a select committee.
Only a few had been chosen to serve. In my own little world,
it had an element of fame and honor. After I agreed, I realized
what kind of business would actually be conducted on that
committee. It was important, but not for me. I was out of
place. Others could more fruitfully serve. I quickly and apolo-
getically resigned. I had to admit I had chosen the prestige of
the appointment before I had checked with those involved to
determine the true extent of the commitment.

3. *Never make a decision under crowd pressure.* Seldom do
we make good choices between greatness and fame while in
the midst of the crowd. It is best to postpone such decisions
to another time. We, like Pilate, try hard to please people. The
air looks much clearer if we wait a day or two.

Suppose you are sitting with your friends in a relaxed atmosphere. Ideas begin to flow. Then, one in the group stands and
proposes that you be appointed chairman to organize and carry
out one of the ideas you have proposed. Everyone in the room
chimes in his agreement. They urge you to do it. At that point
you have several choices.

You could instantly accept the responsibility. Being the
"man of the hour" is invigorating. It is hard not to give in to

popular demand, especially from friends or spiritual people who seem to be giving you the Lord's direction. You could accept out of pure pride. There is a sense in which they have politely told you to "put up or shut up."

You could vehemently decline or suggest someone else for the job. You might be a talker, not a doer, and recognize that you got yourself in over your head. Or you might decline because you are unsure of your gifts and talents. It is better to say no, you think to yourself, than to try and fail.

Or you could genuinely thank the group for their confidence and ask if you could have some time to think and pray about such a serious matter. Most people will grant that courtesy. Return the courtesy by telling them a date you will let them know your decision.

4. *Make sure the decision you make is right in the sight of God, of others, and of yourself.* Does God's Word say anything about the matter? Just because people in town are urging you to attend X-rated films at the theater, does not mean you should do it. Just because everyone in your home Bible study group is convinced you should be elected a deacon, does not mean you should be. Just because everyone in your class says you should design the booth at the school fair, does not mean you should.

Some things are just plain scripturally wrong. Take the X-rated movies, for instance. They are wrong, no matter who is urging you. There are many other things the Bible tells us are wrong, if we take time to investigate. A good knowledge of the Bible is mandatory for anyone who considers finding spiritual greatness.

The Bible also has a lot to say about qualifications for elders and deacons. You would want to consider those carefully.

Perhaps your choice is on the order of the booth at the fair. That would not be specifically mentioned in Scripture, but there are many general principles of leadership and relationships that should be kept in mind. Whatever the subject, in order to determine if the decision is right with God and His revealed Word may take time in prayer and study.

The decision must also be right with others. We do not always stand at the crossroads with a crowd cheering us on. Many times we stand alone. Seek out others who may be involved and see if their decision matches yours.

Finally, the decision must be right with yourself. Is this the general direction in which the Lord has been leading you? Is it compatible with what you know of His will in other areas of your life? Can you do it with a clear conscience?

5. *Consult trusted, faithful, uninvolved people.* In Galatians 2 Paul tells how he traveled to Jerusalem to have the apostles there check out his preaching and doctrine just in case "I might be running, or had run, in vain." Some important decisions require us to consult with a person removed from the scene to see if the whole idea makes sense to him. What kind of person should you seek out?

- One who has no direct involvement with the situation or anything to gain personally by your choice
- One you feel confident has a mature relationship with the Lord and a good understanding of Scripture
- One who knows you well enough to know your strengths and weaknesses
- One who will give you an honest answer, regardless

If you have friends like that, hang on to them. They will turn out to be one of your greatest assets in your quest for success with a purpose.

6. *Decide which direction to take.* Indecision is powerless discipleship. Jesus knew that on-again, off-again decisions were useless. "No one, after putting his hand to the plow and looking back, is fit for the kingdom of God" (Luke 9:62). Radical discipleship includes giving yourself wholeheartedly to the task at hand. Sitting around trying to determine if you have made the right decision or not is a sure sign of coming failure.

In Acts 16 Luke and the others traveling with Paul are awakened to hear that Paul has made a decision, based on a vision, to take the gospel to Europe. Luke records, "Immediately we sought to go into Macedonia, concluding that God had called us to preach the gospel to them."

The decision had been made. No time was wasted in looking back.

7. *Be singleminded in your determination to carry out the task.* "But this one thing I do; forgetting what lies behind and reaching forward to what lies ahead, I press on toward the goal for the prize of the upward call of God in Christ Jesus" (Philippians 3:13-14).

We must learn to be singleminded people. "This one thing I do"—what is the one thing you do? Make your decision. Keep it before you. Then press on, ignoring the distractions of lesser sights along the way.

Lynn decided after prayerful consideration that the Lord was calling her to be a missionary. It seemed to be confirmed by all those around her. She took missionary training and returned home during the summer to make her final plans to leave. But she did not go. She decided to take eight months out of her previous plans to learn to be a hairdresser. She still thinks of herself as a missionary—someday—but first, a little cosmetology.

Be hard-core in your singlemindedness for the Lord. You will get a lot more done.

8. *Be prepared to defend your position.* If you have gone through all those steps and feel strongly you are on the right track, then keep going even under opposition. Your decisions will not always win popular acclaim. You're in good company; Jesus did not find His decisions very popular at times. He was opposed by His mother and brothers, His close disciples, and the religious leaders of the day. So be it. He was right. They were wrong.

Paul tells us about the time he was forced to stand up to Peter in Antioch. Peter was wrong about his relationship to the Gentiles. It is not a hot-tempered Paul trying to assert himself in Galatians 2:11-14, but rather one who knew he was right and was willing to say so.

If you have carefully reasoned out your decision ahead of time and fully sought the Lord's approval, then you are armed with weapons of defense. If you have made a spur-of-the-moment decision, you might not be prepared for the questioning.

Jesus warned us that we could expect opposition. In fact, if you have never had any opposition, you might wonder whether you are even on the right track. A successful spiritual ministry will, of necessity, draw out the resistance of Satan.

9. *Do not retreat.* There is no way to discover if a pathway leads to greatness—success with a purpose—unless you complete every step along the way. Some things take a long, long time.

We live in an instant age. We expect everything to happen at once. We are even impatient to wait the eight seconds for the television to warm up. There is no room for a radical disciple to be impatient. You have signed on to see it through, and nothing is going to keep you from it. It would be sad to count the number of failures that stopped just one corner short of success.

Jim made a pledge to his prayer partner that by next Monday he would talk to Ken about the Lord. He knew that Ken was searching for something secure in life. Three times during the week he lined up times to meet with Ken, but each time Ken called to excuse himself. By Monday Jim was discouraged. He would have to admit to his partner that he had failed. On his way to the Bible study he drove by Ken's house, sure that he would be at work. But his car was parked out front.

Jim stopped and found Ken recovering from a cold. Jim stayed to share Jesus Christ with him. As they talked the doorbell rang. Two callers from his friendly neighborhood cult stood there. Ken sent them on their way. When he returned he said, "You know, Jim, if you hadn't been here I probably would have let them in. I really need someone to talk to."

Jim carried his decision to the last step. Maybe, just maybe, it had eternal significance.

10. *Accept the outcome of your actions as God's will for*

your life. The outcome of your decision might not be exactly as you planned. It might not even resemble your original plans at all. But you have carefully decided what to do, felt certain of the Lord's leading, and carried out the decision to its completion. Now relax and accept the outcome. Your job was to carry out the task. It is God's role to bring the results.

Paul did not always do things perfectly. He knew he had made many mistakes. Yet near the end of his life he could say humbly and with confidence, "I have fought the good fight, I have finished the course, I have kept the faith; in the future there is laid up for me the crown of righteousness, which the Lord, the righteous Judge, will award to me on that day; and not only to me, but also to all who have loved His appearing" (2 Timothy 4:7-8).

Do you remember Frank and Marsha and Bob and Sheila? It is possible that they could have been much more careful about making their decision for a professional music ministry, could have followed each of the prescribed steps exactly, and still have had the same outcome. What difference would it make?

First, they could rest in the confidence that they had truly followed God's leading.

Second, they would be free from guilt feelings that they had in some way disobeyed God.

Third, they would be able to respond much more quickly whenever God might want to lead them again.

Accept the results of your actions as God's will.

Fame or Greatness Checklist
___

   1. Have you taken time to gather all the facts available before deciding? Yes ( ) No ( )

   2. Do the people involved in this decision agree that your facts are accurate? Yes ( ) No ( )

   3. Did you remove yourself from the crowd and its pressure to make a prayerful decision? Yes ( ) No ( )

4. Are you sure that the decision is right in the eyes of God, others, yourself? Yes (   ) No (   )

5. Have you checked with a trusted friend who agrees with your decision? Yes (   ) No (   )

6. Are you willing to make this decision with no reservations or escape clauses? Yes (   ) No (   )

7. Are you willing to set aside every distraction until the task is completed? Yes (   ) No (   )

8. Are you willing and able to defend your decision against critics? Even if they are relatives, friends? Yes (   ) No (   )

9. Are you willing to carry out the task to the final step? Yes (   ) No (   )

10. Do you really feel ready to accept the outcome of your action as God's will for you? Yes (   ) No (   )

17

The Humility of Greatness

God deserves great children. All fathers desire a certain amount of success from their offspring. Our Father in heaven is a great and successful God; we should bear the family resemblance. If that is so, how can we be satisfied with lesser lives when we have the power and opportunity for greatness?

The drawback to this, as you have known from the beginning, is that greatness indicates success. Success often leads to self-pride. And self-pride diminishes the glory that should go to God, therefore drastically reducing any true value to the success we might achieve.

The problem is, How can we achieve greatness that produces true humility in us and also gives honor to God? The last two verses in Mark can help us.

Before His resurrection, Jesus' disciples were an average group of hangers-on. After His resurrection they ministered with power. Even with such instant success they remained humble and continually gave glory for their ministry to the Lord. After the miracle of healing the lame beggar (Acts 3), Peter and John insisted, "Why do you marvel at this, or why do you gaze at us, as if by our own power or piety we had made him walk? The God of Abraham, Isaac, and Jacob, the God of our fathers, has glorified His Servant Jesus . . . and on the basis of faith in His name, it is the name of Jesus which has strengthened this man whom you see and know."

Peter could accept no glory or honor because the miracle was not a result of his power nor his holy living. That is not to say Peter lived an unholy life; it is just that greatness has more to do with the direct action of God than it does with holy living. Peter knew that God and he could do anything.

He was also a successful preacher. In Acts 10 at the home of Cornelius the centurion, he preached, and the whole household was converted. How did the Lord keep Peter from being too puffed up? The household believed *before* Peter even finished his sermon. God and Peter can convert anyone, even with an incomplete sermon. The point is, Peter was totally dependent upon the Lord for any greatness he might achieve, and he knew it very well.

Up to this point we have been studying procedures, step-by-step, for achieving greatness—that is, success with a purpose. Now in the last chapter of the book, we have to throw in a "ringer." You could do all those things mentioned and still not find greatness. Greatness, that deep, satisfying spiritual success and fulfillment, is a *reward* of faithful living, not a result of it. We do not live a certain way, nor do we follow scriptural principles so that God will *have* to grant us success. We cannot put such pressure on Him.

Do we just sit idle, then, and let Him sprinkle greatness upon those whom He arbitrarily chooses? That is not what He has in mind. Suppose that the particular ministry you are involved with could be charted. It might look something like this:

God's Part   *My Part*

———————————————————————— / ————

Now, with such a minor role, can you claim all the honor and glory? Hardly. You could truthfully say you filled in only the minor parts. It is still God's design that you do your part. His plan is to use common, ordinary, forgiven sinners like you and me to complete His work. He will not do it all Himself. Therefore, we strive to obey the principles of Scripture, some of which are mentioned in this book. That is our part. He will do the rest.

The amazing thing is that He allows us to share the victory with Him. That is when we taste true greatness. You might play an insignificant role on a professional football team, yet when your team wins the game, even though you only played two minutes, you are a Super Bowl champion.

Now we are aware of some of the things we need to be busy doing, but what things can we count on Him for? Mark 16: 19-20 helps us out here. There are three things Jesus is going to do for the disciples. He was "received up into heaven, and sat down at the right hand of God" (v. 19). What does that mean? It sounds more like the withdrawing of help. Not true.

Jesus' role in heaven is different from His role here on earth. He is the extension of power of the Father. He sits at the Father's right hand. We are reminded of Christ's role in our prayer life.

> Christ Jesus is He who died, yes, rather who was raised, who is at the right hand of God, who also intercedes for us. [Romans 8:34]

> Hence, also, He is able to save forever those who draw near to God through Him, since He always lives to make intercession for them. [Hebrews 7:25]

> My little children, I am writing these things to you that you may not sin. And if anyone sins, we have an Advocate with the Father, Jesus Christ the righteous. [1 John 2:1]

Jesus is always praying for us. Even when we completely fail to obey God, we still have Him on our side. When we are so overwhelmed we do not even know what to say, we have Jesus praying for us. He promises to be our personal Intercessor and Advocate. How is that for a prayer partner? Can you imagine the Father's not granting the Son a request? Neither can I.

What is Jesus praying for? In what way can He help His disciples? Peter's denial of Jesus is clear in all our minds. We know that Peter repented. He later became one of the most powerful of the postresurrection apostles. Could he brag that he had "seen the light" and repented? No. In Luke 22:31-32 Jesus says, "Simon [Peter], Simon, behold, Satan had demanded permission to sift you like wheat; but I have prayed for you, that your faith may not fail, and you, when once you have turned again, strengthen your brothers."

Can I boast about any sermon I preach when it was all dependent upon the prayers and intercession of Jesus? If He had not sought the Father's forgiveness on my behalf, if He had not asked that Satan be held in check, if He had not asked that the Holy Spirit minister through such an impure vessel, where would my sermon be? All I can do is give glory to the Father and humble thanks to the Son.

A second thing Jesus promised to do for the disciples is found in Mark 16:20: "The Lord worked with them." How can that be? If He is up there in heaven praying for us, how can He be down here working with us? We must remember that when Jesus passed from death to life, from earth to heaven, from the confines of time to eternity, He stepped outside our human limits. He cannot be contained in some isolated prayer closet in heaven. He is still able to personally work with each disciple.

I love that phrase "He worked with them." Jesus does not plan to do everything on His own. If that were God's idea, Jesus would have stayed here on earth, even after the resurrection. He wants us to carry on His ministry. But, we do not do it alone. Remember the closing words of Matthew 28, where Jesus tells His followers, "And lo, I am with you always, even to the end of the age."

Do you remember your first day on a new job? There is a certain amount of apprehension, especially if you are unsure how to carry out your responsibilities. How comforting it is to have some "old pro" come along and say, "Don't worry, kid, I'll work with you." That is exactly what Jesus is saying to you and me. There is no job, task, or ministry that you have to do alone. No matter how overwhelming the prospect, no matter how disproportioned the odds against you, you have a guarantee of help from the Lord Himself.

Think carefully about the kind of help you get. If you did not know how to build a house, you would want a carpenter to help. If you did not know how to speak a language, you would want a bilingual teacher to help. If you did not know how to file your tax forms, you would want an accountant to help. How about finding true spiritual greatness? Who could be better help than Jesus Christ? That is exactly the kind of assistance He promises every disciple.

A third role Jesus promised to fill in our lives is that of confirming our words and deeds. Mark 16:20 states: "And [Jesus] confirmed the word by the signs that followed." We immediately think of the dramatic signs and miracles that happened often during the ministry of the apostles. You might not have a ministry of dramatic miracles, but Jesus is still in the business of confirming our work for Him.

That confirmation shows we are on the right track. It is possible for us as His disciples to *know* that we are doing His will, engaged in the work that He has prepared for us. There is always a tendency for us to wonder, "Am I truly doing the Lord's will?" We are too close to the influence of our own wills and motives, which control even important decisions, so doubts creep in. We constantly question ourselves. We want to know for sure. We want some divine orders to float down on royal stationery with our names on it.

He has promised to confirm our ministries. Notice that the confirmation for the apostles did not come before they began to obey His call, but after it. Jesus sent Peter out to be a preacher, but that preaching was not confirmed until after the sermon was delivered. In Acts 2:41 we learn that three thousand people accepted the Lord after Peter's first sermon. That is pretty solid confirmation!

Our confirmations might not be as dramatic, but certainly they can be as solid. Recently our church saw the need to establish a Bible-school-caliber course. It would mean the purcase of expensive video equipment. We wanted to know whether it was really the Lord's will. We knew we needed thirty people who were serious enough about the course to do advance study, outside reading, weekly assignments, and exams. So we publicized the course. On the closing day of registration we had forty-one people signed up. We felt that the Lord confirmed our proposed ministry. It was just the affirmation we needed to proceed with plans for the Bible school.

Debbie was getting tired. It had been a long, hot summer and the children were restless. She had taught this fifth and sixth grade Sunday school class for six years. What usually was her pride and joy was now a "drag," yet she was so attached to the class she could not imagine giving it up. She needed some confirmation whether that was still what the Lord wanted her to do. She prayed and prayed. All through July and Angust, through the Sunday school picnic, and through vacation Bible school she prayed. She did not hear anything until one Sunday evening in September. During the worship service Mike stood to tell of his decision to go to a Christian college because he wanted to give his life in service to God.

Mike was a bright, active, and popular high school senior. He loved sports, any kind, any time. Yet there was something deeper. He had a hard time telling the congregation such personal things, though he knew he had to. As Mike sat down the pastor asked him what was the turning point that brought him to the decision of seeking full-time Christian service. "Oh," he said, "I owe it all to the Lord and Mrs. Sedgwick. She led me to Him in the sixth grade, and He has never let go of me since." Debbie Sedgwick had all the confirmation she needed.

Maria Martinez returned home from church with her thoughts heavy from the sermon she had heard. It had been from Matthew 5 about "giving to those who ask." The preacher had made the point of exposing the affluence and attachment we have to the material goods of the world. As Maria hung up her dress she noticed how crowded her closet was. It was all she could do to find room for the stylish blue suit. She felt she wanted to give, but nobody was asking. Convicted by the Lord, she prayed, "Lord, if anyone asks, help make me willing to give up some of these beautiful clothes."

By Wednesday she had almost forgotten that prayer. After all, no one had asked her—not until Thursday. She read in the paper about a fire that destroyed all the belongings of a family of fairly new immigrants in town. The last line in the article said, "Mr. and Mrs. Perez are in great need of clothing for themselves and their children. Anyone wishing to contribute may bring things to La Colonia Community Center."

Maria Martinez had her confirmation. Someone was asking. She just needed to respond. For just a moment she wished she had prayed about giving the old clothes in the barrel out in the garage. But she had offered her good clothes, so off to the closet she went. She divided everything into two equally adequate wardrobes. She would have been happy to keep either; she really wanted to keep both. But she neatly boxed one of them and took them to the community center. The following Sunday she wore the same suit as the week before, but Maria never looked prettier.

Jesus will confirm our ministries. There is an important factor in His confirming our work and ministries. That is, we do not have the responsibility of proving the validity of our ministries. That is important. It is not my job as a preacher, for instance, to convince everyone that my words are from the Lord. It is His job to do the convincing. I do not have to stand in the pulpit and say, "Now everybody should listen to me because the Lord told me to tell you these things." All I need to do is preach. He will do the rest.

That is good news because I am not cut out to be a salesman. Even if I were, I do not want anyone to purchase anything. I want those who hear me to know God, to love Him, and desire to serve Him. So I preach and He confirms. I do the easy part and He the difficult part. I like it that way. He will prove the validity of your ministry too. It is His business.

Once we are fully able to grasp the significance of the Lord's active, personal help in everything we attempt for Him, we can never get puffed up with pride. Is it any point of pride for me to say, "Bev Shea and I can sing better than you"? Or, "Billy Graham and I can draw larger crowds than you"? Or, "World Vision and I can feed more hungry people than you"? Such statements are ridiculous. So is the idea that we could ever boast of our own greatness. Great people of God have always been overwhelmed with their own unworthiness to be in the position God has placed them in.

The eighty-year-old man on the hillside complained to the Lord God that he was not adequate for such a large task. "Who am I, that I should go to Pharaoh, and that I should bring the sons of Israel out of Egypt?" Yet, Moses was the one God wanted (see Exodus 3).

The young man spent his life dedicated to all the observances of the priesthood. Yet when he found himself face-to-face with Almighty God, it was all he could do to stammer, "Woe is me, for I am ruined. Because I am a man of unclean lips." Yet, it was Isaiah that the Lord wanted to proclaim His prophetic word (see Isaiah 6).

Another man taught, preached, exhorted, and encouraged people throughout the whole known world. He was the one God chose to almost singlehandedly lead Christianity out of being a provincial Jewish sect, to make it a faith of world-wide significance. He undoubtedly had, and still has, more influence on Christians than any person other than Jesus Christ. Yet how did he see himself? Paul said, "I am the chief of all sinners" (see 1 Timothy 1:15). True spiritual greatness, success with a purpose, produces sincere humility before God.

Why should you want to achieve greatness? Here are four reasons.

1. *You will be able to bring more glory to God.* The more true spiritual success you achieve, the more praise and honor will go to Him. Isn't that what you really desire?

2. *You will experience the abundant life that has been promised.* Abundance, that is, life lived to its very fullest, is the birthright of every believer. Yet it is actually enjoyed by only a few who venture out on the trail of spiritual greatness.

3. *You will find spiritual satisfaction.* That is a certain integrity of spirit, a feeling that we have truly given our all to the Lord. That satisfaction has nothing to do with the acclaim of the world. We can be, and most of us will be, unknown people of God. Yet if you and I finish our terms on earth with the

knowledge that we have given our best, we can stand with Paul and proclaim, we have "fought the good fight, finished the course, kept the faith" (2 Timothy 4:7).

4. *You will find you have a magnificent crown in heaven.* Paul tells us, "In the future there is laid up for me the crown of righteousness" (2 Timothy 4:8).

Does it sound odd to say that you should push out to achieve greatness because it might affect your reward or crown in heaven? What can you do with a crown in heaven? Here is one thing.

> The twenty-four elders will fall down before Him who sits on the throne, and will worship Him who lives forever and ever, and *will cast their crowns before the throne,* saying, 'Worthy art Thou, our Lord and our God, to receive glory and honor and power; for Thou didst create all things, and because of Thy will they existed, and were created [Revelation 4:10-11, italics added].

Lord, I want to be in that number. I want to be there with crown in hand as we worship face-to-face the Lord of Lords and King of Kings.

If humility is the hallmark of true spiritual greatness, then any thought of personal recognition is fool's play. It is only the Lord's graciousness that allows us to share in His victory. But He truly wants us to share. He is urging all believers to press on to achieve greatness. To us and to us alone He has granted the right to taste success with a spiritual, lasting, meaningful, satisfying purpose.

Lord, I just want to be great.